AQA STUDY GUIDE

GCSE 9–1
BLOOD OOD
BROTHERS

BY WILLY RUSSELL

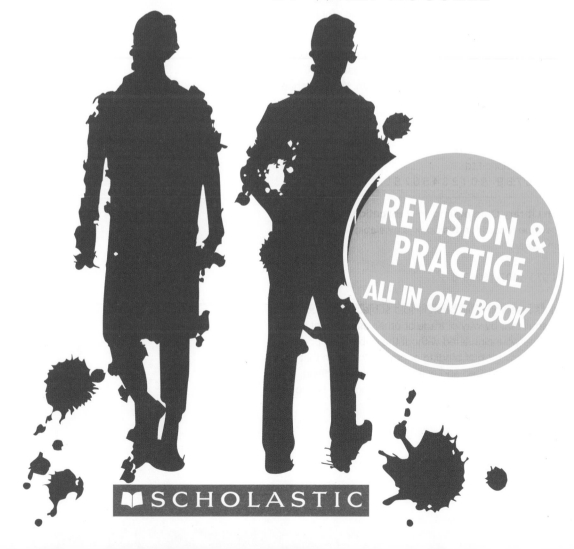

REVISION & PRACTICE
ALL IN ONE BOOK

SCHOLASTIC

Authors Richard Durant and Cindy Torn

Series Consultants Richard Durant and Cindy Torn

Reviewer Rob Pollard

Editorial team Rachel Morgan, Audrey Stokes, Camilla Erskine, Lesley Densham, Anne Henwood, Louise Titley

Typesetting Oxford Designers & Illustrators Ltd

Cover design Nicolle Thomas and Neil Salt

App development Hannah Barnett, Phil Crothers and Haremi Ltd

Acknowledgements
Bloomsbury Publishing Plc for the use of extracts from *Blood Brothers* by Willy Russell. Text (c) 1985, Willy Russell, (2017, Methuen Drama, an imprint of Bloomsbury Publishing Plc)

Illustration Ai Higaki/Oxford Designers & Illustrators

Photographs page 4: book cover image, © Bloomsbury Publishing Plc; pages 12, 51 and 63: smoking gun, Maksym Dykha/Shutterstock; page 13: milk bottle, Winston Link/Shutterstock; page 45: rose, Hong Vo/Shutterstock; page 51: pills, Dima Sobko/Shutterstock; page 63: catapult, Photo One/Shutterstock; page 64, tragedy mask, A.B.G./Shutterstock; page 73: Margaret Thatcher, Paul Marriott/Alamy; page 78: Marilyn Monroe, Shawshots/Alamy; pages 81 and 82: stage sets by Ruth Neeman; page 90: girl sitting exam, Monkey Business Images/Shutterstock; page 93: notepad and pen, TRINACRIA PHOTO/Shutterstock

Designed using Adobe InDesign

Published by Scholastic Education, an imprint of Scholastic Ltd, Book End, Range Road, Witney, Oxfordshire, OX29 0YD
Registered office: Westfield Road, Southam, Warwickshire CV47 0RA
www.scholastic.co.uk

Printed by Bell and Bain
© 2019 Scholastic Ltd
1 2 3 4 5 6 7 8 9 9 0 1 2 3 4 5 6 7 8

British Library Cataloguing-in-Publication Data
A catalogue record for this book is available from the British Library.

ISBN 978-1407-18263-6

Contents

Check your answers on the free revision app or at www.scholastic.co.uk/gcse

How to use this book

This Study Guide is designed to help you prepare effectively for your AQA GCSE English literature exam question on *Blood Brothers* (Paper 2, Section A).

The content has been organised in a sequence that builds confidence, and which will deepen your knowledge and understanding of the play step by step. Therefore, it is best to work through this book in the order that it is presented.

HOW TO REVISE!

This Study Guide uses the Methuen Drama Student edition (Bloomsbury).

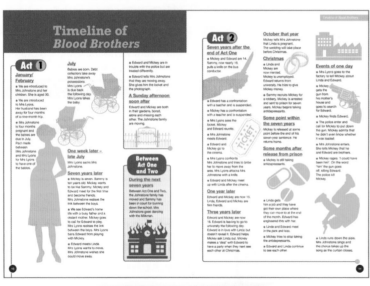

Know the plot

1 It is very important that you know the plot well: to be clear about what happens and in what order. The **timeline** on pages 10–11 provides a useful overview of the plot, highlighting key events.

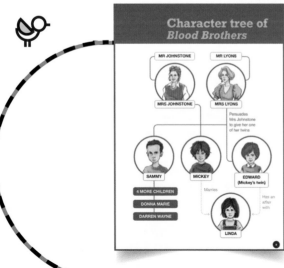

The **character tree** on page 9 introduces you to the main characters of the text.

The chronological section

2 The chronological section on pages 12–57 takes you through the play scene by scene, providing plot summaries and pointing out important details. It is also designed to help you think about the structure of the play.

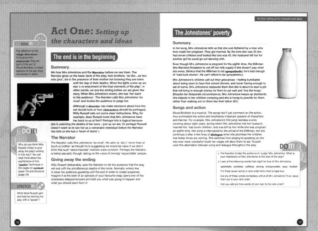

This section provides an in-depth exploration of themes or character development, drawing your attention to how Russell's language choices reveal the play's meaning.

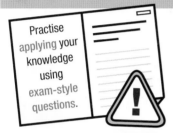

Practise applying your knowledge using exam-style questions.

The play as a whole

3 The second half of the guide is retrospective: it helps you to look back over the whole play through a number of relevant 'lenses': characters, themes, Russell's language, forms and structural features.

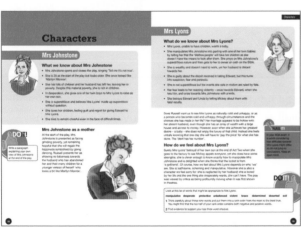

Doing well in your AQA Exam

Stick to the **TIME LIMITS** you will need to in the exam.

4 Finally, you will find an extended 'Doing well in your AQA exam' section which guides you through the process of understanding questions, and planning and writing answers.

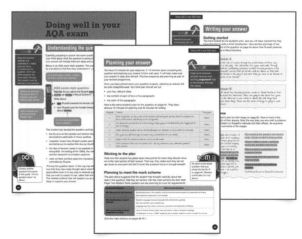

Features of this guide

The best way to retain information is to take an active approach to revision.

Throughout this book, you will find lots of features that will make your revision an active, successful process.

SNAPIT!

Use the Snap it! feature in the revision app to take pictures of key concepts and information. Great for revision on the go!

DEFINEIT!

Explains the meaning of difficult words from the set texts.

Callouts Additional explanations of important points.

words shown in **purple** **bold** can be found in the glossary on pages 94–95

Find methods of relaxation that work for you throughout the revision period.

Regular exercise helps stimulate the brain and will help you relax.

DOIT!

Activities to embed your knowledge and understanding and prepare you for the exams.

NAILIT!

Succinct and vital tips on how to do well in your exam.

STRETCHIT!

Provides content that stretches you further.

REVIEW IT!

Helps you to consolidate and understand what you have learned before moving on.

Revise in pairs or small groups and deliver presentations on topics to each other.

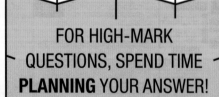

FOR HIGH-MARK QUESTIONS, SPEND TIME **PLANNING** YOUR ANSWER!

AQA exam-style question

AQA exam-style sample questions based on the extract shown are given on some pages. Use the sample mark scheme on page 86 to help you assess your responses. This will also help you understand what you could do to improve your response.

FREE REVISION APP

- The **free revision app** can be downloaded to your mobile phone (iOS and Android), making **on-the-go revision** easy.

- Use the revision calendar to help map out your revision in the lead-up to the exam.

- Complete multiple-choice questions and create your own SNAP**IT!** revision cards.

www.scholastic.co.uk/gcse

Online answers and additional resources
All of the tasks in this book are designed to get you thinking and to consolidate your understanding through thought and application. Therefore, it is important to write your own answers before checking. Some questions include tables where you need to fill in your answer in the book. Other questions require you to use a separate piece of paper so that you can draft your response and work out the best way of answering.

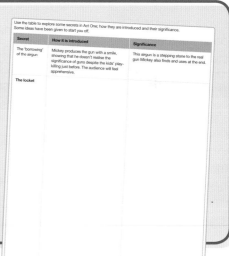

Get plenty of sleep, especially the night before an exam.

LOOK AFTER YOURSELF

Help your brain by looking after your whole body!

Once you have worked through a section, you can check your answers to Do it!, Stretch it!, Review it! and the exam practice sections on the app or at **www.scholastic.co.uk/gcse**.

Why study *Blood Brothers*?

Although *Blood Brothers* was written well before you were born, it has kept its appeal for today's audiences. The subject matter of the play still has a strong relevance. Two children – Mickey and Edward – are born to the same mother on the same day and are separated a few days later. They share the same genes but they are brought up in different conditions. One grows up in poverty, the other in well-off comfort. One is successful in education and becomes a businessman and a respected councillor; the other slumps into depression, crime and marginal employment. The play dramatically shows that who and what we become can be a matter of luck, not natural talent. Or – to put it more simply – life just isn't fair.

Another dramatic feature of *Blood Brothers* is secret bonds and their dangers. Many modern teenagers have kept secrets from their parents – including secret relationships. Sometimes these relationships are kept secret to avoid parents' disapproval, sometimes a disapproval based on snobbery. The plot of *Blood Brothers* gives powerful expression to all these familiar feelings, experiences and attitudes. The plot's constant focus on conflict and the struggle for justice will surely strike a chord with many teenagers.

Blood Brothers in your AQA exam

Blood Brothers is examined in Section A (the first part) of the second AQA GCSE English Literature exam, Paper 2 Modern prose or drama. Here is how it fits into the overall assessment framework:

Paper 1 Time: **1 hour 45 minutes**	Paper 2 Time: **2 hours 15 minutes**
Section A: Shakespeare	**Section A: Modern prose or drama:** ***Blood Brothers***
Section B: 19th-century novel	Section B: Poetry anthology
	Section C: Unseen poetry

There will be two questions on *Blood Brothers*. You must answer **one** of them. You should spend **45 minutes** planning and writing your answer to the question. There are 30 marks available for the *Blood Brothers* question, plus four extra marks for good **vocabulary, spelling, sentences and punctuation** (VSSP, sometimes called 'SPaG').

A character tree

The 'character tree' on page 9 should help you to fix in your mind the names of the characters, their relationships and who did what to whom.

Timeline of Blood Brothers

The timeline on pages 10–11 provides a visual overview of the plot, highlighting key events which take place over the course of the play. It will also help you to think about the structure of the play.

Character tree of *Blood Brothers*

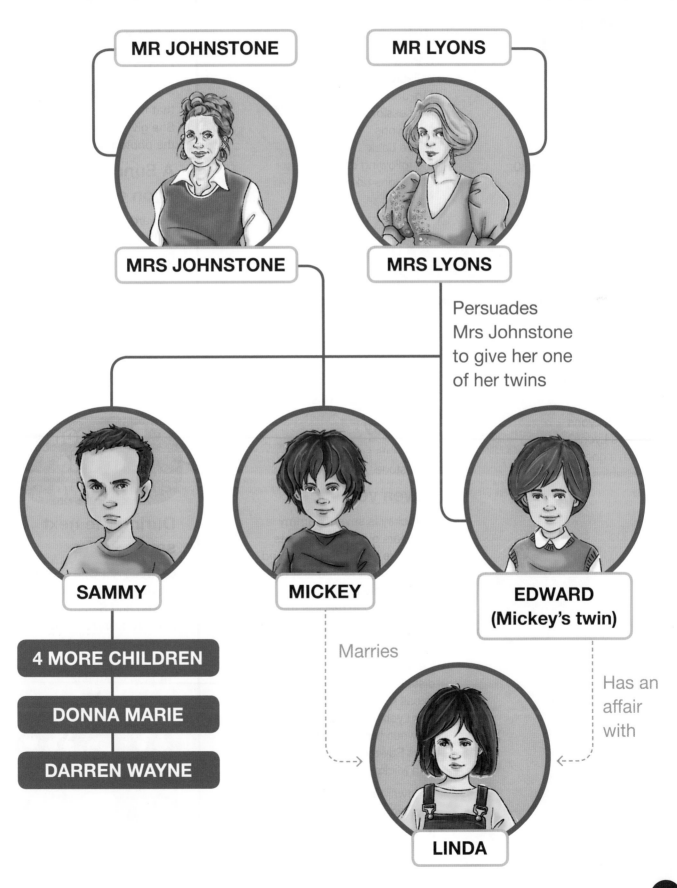

MR JOHNSTONE

MR LYONS

MRS JOHNSTONE

MRS LYONS

Persuades Mrs Johnstone to give her one of her twins

SAMMY

MICKEY

EDWARD
(Mickey's twin)

4 MORE CHILDREN

DONNA MARIE

DARREN WAYNE

Marries

Has an affair with

LINDA

Timeline of *Blood Brothers*

Act 1

January/ February

✻ We are introduced to Mrs Johnstone and her children. She is aged 30.

✻ We are introduced to Mrs Lyons. Her husband has been away for four months of a nine-month trip.

✻ Mrs Johnstone is four months pregnant and the babies are due in July. Pact made between Mrs Johnstone and Mrs Lyons for Mrs Lyons to have one of the babies.

July

Babies are born. Debt collectors take away Mrs Johnstone's possessions. Mrs Lyons is due back the following day. Mrs Lyons takes the baby.

One week later – late July

Mrs Lyons sacks Mrs Johnstone.

Seven years later

✻ Mickey is seven. Sammy is ten years old. Mickey wants to be like Sammy. Mickey and Edward meet for the first time and become friends. Mrs Johnstone realises the link between the boys.

✻ We see Edward's home life with a busy father and a distant mother. Mickey goes to call for Edward to play. Mrs Lyons realises the link between the boys. Mrs Lyons bans Edward from playing with Mickey.

✻ Edward meets Linda. Mrs Lyons wants to move. Mrs Johnstone wishes she could move away.

✻ Edward and Mickey are in trouble with the police but are treated differently.

✻ Edward tells Mrs Johnstone that they are moving away. She gives him the locket and the photograph.

A Sunday afternoon soon after

Edward and Mickey are both in their gardens, bored, alone and missing each other. The Johnstone family are moving.

Between Act One and Two

During the next seven years

Between Act One and Two, the Johnstone family has moved and Sammy has been in court for burning down the school. Mrs Johnstone goes dancing with the Milkman.

10

Act 2

Seven years after the end of Act One

✳ Mickey and Edward are 14. Sammy, now nearly 16, pulls a knife on the bus conductor.

✳ Edward has a confrontation with a teacher and is suspended.

✳ Mickey has a confrontation with a teacher and is suspended.

✳ Mrs Lyons sees the locket. Mickey and Edward reunite.

✳ Mrs Johnstone meets Edward.

✳ Edward and Mickey go to the cinema.

✳ Mrs Lyons confronts Mrs Johnstone and tries to bribe her to move away from the area. Mrs Lyons attacks Mrs Johnstone with a knife.

✳ Edward and Mickey meet up with Linda after the cinema.

One year later

Edward and Mickey are now 15. Linda, Edward and Mickey are firm friends.

Three years later

Edward and Mickey are now 18. Edward is leaving to go to university the following day. Edward is in love with Linda but doesn't reveal it. Edward helps Mickey ask Linda out. Mickey makes a 'deal' with Edward to have a party when they next see each other at Christmas.

October that year

Mickey tells Mrs Johnstone that Linda is pregnant. The wedding will take place before Christmas.

Christmas

✳ Linda and Mickey are now married. Mickey is unemployed. Edward returns from university. He tries to give Mickey money.

✳ Sammy recruits Mickey for a robbery. Mickey is arrested and sent to prison for seven years. Mickey begins taking antidepressants.

Some point within the seven years

Mickey is released at some point before the end of his seven-year sentence. He returns home.

Some months after release from prison

✳ Mickey is still taking antidepressants.

✳ Linda gets him a job and they have got their own place where they can move to at the end of the month. Edward has engineered this with her.

✳ Linda and Edward meet in the park and kiss.

✳ Mickey tries to stop taking the antidepressants.

✳ Edward and Linda continue to see each other.

Events of one day

✳ Mrs Lyons goes to the factory to tell Mickey about Linda and Edward.

✳ Mickey gets the gun from his mother's house and goes to search for Edward.

✳ Mickey finds Edward.

✳ The police enter and call for Mickey to put down the gun. Mickey admits that he didn't even know whether it was loaded.

✳ Mrs Johnstone enters. She tells Mickey that he and Edward are brothers.

✳ Mickey rages: 'I could have been him'. On the word 'him' the gun goes off, killing Edward. The police kill Mickey.

✳ Linda runs down the aisle. Mrs Johnstone sings and the chorus takes up the song as the curtain closes.

Act One: *Setting up the characters and ideas*

NAILIT!

Pay attention to the **stage directions** throughout the **playscript**: they are part of the text of *Blood Brothers*. In most editions of the play they are printed in *italics*.

The end is in the beginning

Summary

We hear Mrs Johnstone and the **Narrator** before we see them. The Narrator gives us the basic facts of the play: twin brothers, 'as like...as two new pins', die in the presence of their mother not knowing they are twins

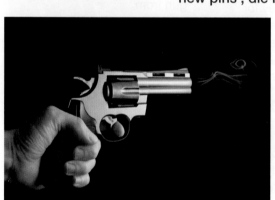

until the day of their deaths. When the lights come up we see '*a re-enactment of the final moments of the play*': in other words, we see the ending before we are given the story. When Mrs Johnstone enters, she has '*her back to the audience*'. The Narrator calls Mrs Johnstone 'so cruel' and invites the audience to judge her.

(Although a **director** can make decisions about how the set should look or how **characters** should be portrayed, Willy Russell sets out some clear instructions. Why, for example, does Russell insist that Mrs Johnstone have her back to us at first? Perhaps this is logical because she is watching the deaths of her sons – just as we are. Or perhaps Russell doesn't want us to see her as a vulnerable individual before the Narrator has told us she has a 'heart of stone'.)

The Narrator

The Narrator calls Mrs Johnstone 'so cruel'. He asks us 'did y' never hear of [such a] mother' as though he is suggesting we would be naive if we didn't think that such 'stone-hearted' mothers were common. Perhaps the Narrator is being sarcastic though, taking on the voice of (wrong) 'respectable' people.

Giving away the ending

Willy Russell deliberately uses the Narrator to tell the audience that the play will end with the simultaneous deaths of the twins. Normally writers like to keep the audience guessing until the end in order to create suspense. Imagine if at the start of an episode of your favourite soap opera one of the characters stepped forward and told you what was going to happen and what you should learn from it!

DOIT!

Why do you think Willy Russell chose to give away the play's ending in this way? You can read more about the significance of this '**spoiler**' technique in the pages on **context** (page 73) and structure (page 79).

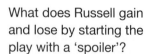
STRETCHIT!

What does Russell gain and lose by starting the play with a 'spoiler'?

The Johnstones' poverty

Summary

In her song, Mrs Johnstone tells us that she was flattered by a man who then made her pregnant. They got married. By the time she was 25 she had seven children and looked like she was 42. Her husband left her for another girl he could go out dancing with.

Even though Mrs Johnstone is pregnant for the eighth time, the Milkman (the Narrator) threatens to cut off her milk supply if she doesn't pay what she owes. (Notice that the Milkman is not **sympathetic**: he's had enough of 'hard luck stories'. He can't afford to be sympathetic.)

Mrs Johnstone's children call out their grievances – feeling humiliated about being seen to have free school dinners, and never having enough to eat at home. Mrs Johnstone reassures them that she is about to start a job that will bring in enough money for them to eat well and 'live like kings'. (Despite her desperate circumstances, Mrs Johnstone keeps up standards: she objects to her children swearing and she is trying to provide for them, rather than walking out on them like their father did.)

Songs and action

Blood Brothers is a musical. The songs don't just comment on the action, they summarise the action and emphasise important aspects of characters and themes. For example, Mrs Johnstone's first song narrates events covering about eight years, during which Mrs Johnstone met her husband, married him, had seven children, and was left by him while she was pregnant an eighth time. Her song is interrupted by the arrival of the Milkman, but she continues it after a few lines of **dialogue** when she promises her children that better times are coming. She switches from singing to speaking as she lists ever more wonderful foods her wages will allow them to eat. Russell uses this alternation between song and dialogue throughout the play.

1 The Narrator invites the audience to 'judge' Mrs Johnstone. What is your impression of Mrs Johnstone at the start of the play?

2 Look at the following words that *might* be true of Mrs Johnstone.

optimistic reckless selfless strong irresponsible sexy foolish

Put these seven words in rank order from most to least true.

Are any of these words completely *un*true of Mrs Johnstone? If so, leave them out of your rank order.

Can you add any true words of your own to the rank order?

The deal is done

Summary

Mrs Johnstone is working as a cleaner for Mrs Lyons, whose husband is away for nine months. Mrs Lyons sadly tells Mrs Johnstone that she and her husband have been unable to have children. Mrs Lyons terrifies Mrs Johnstone by putting a pair of new shoes on the table, which is traditionally believed to bring bad luck. (This moment introduces an important **motif** in the play – bad luck and superstition. The play uses many **symbols** of bad luck, including a single magpie, spilled salt and a broken mirror.)

Mrs Johnstone is dismayed to discover from the Gynaecologist (the Narrator again) that she is carrying twins. Mrs Johnstone asks Mrs Johnstone to give her one of the babies: she will pretend it is her own. She persuades her by pointing out that Mrs Johnstone will see her baby every day, and that the baby will be brought up with many advantages.

Mrs Lyons makes Mrs Johnstone swear on the Bible to seal their agreement. Then Mrs Lyons goes out shopping with a concealed cushion as a pregnancy bump, leaving Mrs Johnstone '*afraid*' of what she has done. (Mrs Johnstone is '*uncomfortable*' about the formality of this agreement. She senses that she has been pushed into something that she will regret. The Narrator almost seems to relish her discomfort, dramatically hinting to us that she will regret the agreement.)

Opposites and inequality

Mrs Johnstone and Mrs Lyons are opposites: one is wealthy, the other is poor. However, compared with Mrs Lyons, Mrs Johnstone is rich in one thing: she has a lot of children. Even so, it is their financial inequality that allows Mrs Lyons to exploit Mrs Johnstone. Mrs Lyons can offer 'their' child economic security, and without a ninth mouth to feed, Mrs Johnstone might be able to maintain the other eight.

The differences between the two women are also shown in the way they speak. Willy Russell gives Mrs Johnstone dialogue with 'missed out' letters (for example, 'goin' 'rather than 'going') so that it fits a working-class Liverpool **accent**. Mrs Lyons' dialogue is more careful as though she is (perhaps unconsciously) showing her superiority.

Their agreement is unequal and is sealed over the ominous sound of a '*bass note, repeated as a heartbeat*' that grows in intensity signalling Russell's sense of drama.

DOIT!

Write a paragraph explaining the **effect** on the audience of how the deal is done.

Social inequality

In this section, we clearly see the inequality between social classes and how the social class of your family determines the sort of life chances you can expect.

The song that Mrs Johnstone and Mrs Lyons share highlights these inequalities:

> **MRS JOHNSTONE:**
> If my child was raised
> In a palace like this one,
> (He) wouldn't have to worry where
> His next meal was comin' from.

Calling Mrs Lyons' comfortable, middle-class house 'a palace' is a **hyperbole** that tells us more about the poor housing that Mrs Johnstone's family has to put up with than it does about Mrs Lyons' house. We also learn that the Johnstones' poverty must be very deep if they can't even guarantee that they will be able to eat.

Now Willy Russell puts hyperbole into the mouth of Mrs Lyons to emphasise the contrasts between the two households:

Mrs Lyons' reference to silver trays is a joke, exaggerating how 'posh' the baby's life will be. Mrs Johnstone jokes too by suggesting that having two wheels on your bike is an almost unimaginable luxury. Because the double syllable **rhyme** of 'meals on'/'wheels on' is surprising and delightful, it emphasises the jokes the two women have made.

> **MRS LYONS**: Silver trays to take meals on.
> **MRS JOHNSTONE**: A bike with *both* wheels on?
> **MRS LYONS** *nods enthusiastically.*

> **MRS LYONS**: And he'd sleep every night
> In a bed of his own.
> **MRS JOHNSTONE**: He wouldn't get into fights
> He'd leave matches alone.
> And you'd never find him
> Effin' and blindin'.

Here Mrs Johnstone suggests that the effects of poverty are not just economic: they are social too. Mrs Lyons' twin will not fight, commit arson and swear, which Mrs Johnstone **implies** are normal for a child from a poor family. Her **slang** term for swearing – Effin' and blindin' – further show her working-class identity.

In this section of Act One – and elsewhere – what do you think are the clearest indicators of a character's social class?

Make a list of some of those indicators and where we see them in the play.

STRETCH IT!

Choose two of the indicators from your list and consider how class influences the character's life at that point.

AQA exam-style question

What ideas about social inequality does Russell explore in the play *Blood Brothers*?

Write about:

- how Russell uses different characters and their ideas about social inequality

- how Russell presents these ideas by the ways he writes.

[30 marks]

Poverty and superstition

Summary

Mrs Johnstone returns home with her newborn twins to find debt collectors are removing goods from her house. She realises that nothing is really hers – not even one of her babies – and that there is a price she will always have to pay. (For a poor person like Mrs Johnstone even her baby is not a possession she can definitely keep. She can't keep up the instalment payments on her catalogue items so they have to go back. Similarly, she knows that the 'Welfare' (the authorities) will take away her children if she can't afford to look after them.)

Mrs Johnstone reluctantly hands over one twin to Mrs Lyons who gives her the rest of the week off on full pay. Mrs Johnstone has to tell her children that one of the twins has 'gone up to heaven'.

Back at work, Mrs Johnstone fusses over Mrs Lyons' baby. Worried, Mrs Lyons persuades her husband that Mrs Johnstone should be dismissed. Mrs Lyons accuses Mrs Johnstone of bad work and offers her a 'fifty pound' pay-off. Angered, Mrs Johnson threatens to go to the police, but Mrs Lyons tells her that they will only lock her up for selling her baby. She finally makes Mrs Johnstone leave with the fifty pounds by telling her that if twins who have been parted find out later that they are twins, they will 'both immediately die', and that therefore Mrs Johnstone would have killed them. (In effect, Mrs Lyons has broken the agreement allowing Mrs Johnstone to see her lost twin every day. To force Mrs Johnstone to give up her baby, Mrs Lyons uses her wealth and her class superiority and a frightening superstition about parted twins. Yet earlier Mrs Lyons laughed at Mrs Johnstone for being superstitious.)

Write a paragraph exploring *your reactions* to the two women in this part of the play. Explain which woman you have more sympathy for.

The devil's knocking at your door

The Narrator's song warns that the sale of the baby will bring endless bad luck to Mrs Johnstone. She is now under the control of the devil, who will never go away. The Narrator tells us that it is Mrs Johnstone – not Mrs Lyons – who made a pact with the devil by the sale of a son. The outcome of this pact seems very unequal.

Poverty and working-class life

The debt collectors are embarrassed about taking away all Mrs Johnstone's possessions just as she arrives home with newborn twins.

> **CATALOGUE MAN**: Look, if y' could give me a couple of weeks' money on this I could leave it.
>
> **MRS JOHNSTONE** *shakes her head.*
>
> **FINANCE MAN**: Y' shouldn't have signed for all this stuff, should y'? Y' knew y' wouldn't be able to pay, didn't y'?

The Catalogue Man is sympathetic and feels guilty. He offers Mrs Johnstone a chance to avoid having her goods repossessed. The Finance Man's accusing **tone** suggests that he too is feeling guilty. Both men are from Mrs Johnstone's own class: Willy Russell shows this by the way they speak, using the shortened – y' – for the word 'you'.

Willy Russell seems to be making the point that working-class people do not necessarily stick up for each other. We see this earlier when the Milkman/Narrator refuses to give Mrs Johnstone any more credit and is willing to cut off her milk supply even though she is pregnant. He is forced to put his own survival above another working-class person's needs: 'I'm up to here with hard luck stories,' he tells Mrs Johnstone: there is so much poverty that he cannot afford to be charitable.

Explain briefly to what extent you agree with this student's view of who is to blame *at this point in the play*.

Who's to blame?

Here is a student writing about who is to blame for Mrs Johnstone's desperate circumstances:

> You can't really blame Mrs Lyons because she hasn't caused Mrs Johnstone's poverty and in a way she is helping Mrs Johnstone to cope with poverty. The real culprit is Mr Johnstone for selfishly abandoning Mrs Johnstone and their children, so it's men, not the middle class, who are to blame.

1 After Mrs Johnstone has been paid off, the Narrator enters and tells Mrs Johnstone, now you have sold your son, 'the devil's got your number'. Is he warning or blaming Mrs Johnstone?

2 Read or sing the Narrator's song. Try out different gestures and tones of voice to suggest different ways of **interpreting** the Narrator's attitude.

Character and theme essentials

Poverty and class

Mrs Johnstone becomes poorer with every child she has. She is poor in money but rich in children. Middle-class Mrs Lyons is her reverse image: rich in money but poor in children. Willy Russell seems to suggest that there is more than one way to be poor, and he seems to avoid a simplistic image of a heroic working class being crushed by a greedy upper class (although this is suggested later). We feel sympathy for Mrs Lyons despite her wealth, and it is working-class characters who are cruel to Mrs Johnstone at the beginning of the play – the Milkman who denies milk to a pregnant woman; the heartless Finance Man, and, of course, the husband who puts his own interests before his family's.

Fate and superstition

Mrs Lyons laughs at Mrs Johnstone for being superstitious about putting new shoes on the table, but she uses Mrs Johnstone's superstition against her to finally force her to hand over a twin. Mrs Johnstone seems to put her desperate poverty down to bad luck and fate rather than the selfishness of others. The fact that the play begins with its tragic ending suggests that the events are inevitable. Willy Russell seems to be suggesting that working-class poverty cannot be escaped.

Women, men and family

Both women are committed to their children – either the ones they have got or the ones they wish they had. They are loyal to their families and put their families' interests before their own. However, their men are not equally supportive. Mr Lyons is patronising towards his wife and seems to value his work more than her. Mr Lyons neglects his wife, while Mr Johnstone abandons his completely.

The Narrator

The Narrator takes on a number of roles during the play. He summarises the action and passes comments on the characters, and so he guides our reactions to the play's characters and ideas.

The tone that the Narrator actor uses is important. For example, when he calls Mrs Johnstone 'so cruel', are we supposed to agree with him? Should he sound sarcastic, as though he is quoting the (wrong) views of 'respectable' people who have not had to face her circumstances? Should he sound neutral? Should he sound sympathetic? Different directors and actors will make different decisions.

Mrs Johnstone

Mrs Johnstone has been pregnant eight times by the age of 25 and she looks much older. Although her life has been reduced to a weary struggle to survive, she is a fighter who does not give up. She still dreams and hopes for better times when she can again go dancing and be called as beautiful as Marilyn Monroe. Her husband has abandoned her, yet she shows no bitterness towards him, just sad acceptance. Russell doesn't present her as showing jealousy or resentment.

Mrs Lyons

Mrs Lyons is a well-off, non-working wife living in a house large enough for a family, but she and her husband have been unable to have children and this leaves her feeling empty. She is so desperate for her own child that she uses her advantages and Mrs Johnstone's disadvantages to force Mrs Johnstone to give her one of the twins. Her actions are surely best explained by her desperate unhappiness rather than by her evil. She loves children and wants to give her twin a wonderful upbringing.

REVIEW IT!

1 Where did Mr and Mrs Johnstone meet?

2 How many children did Mrs Johnstone have by the age of 25?

3 What job does Mrs Johnstone get?

4 Why is Mr Lyons unwilling to adopt a child?

5 What does Mrs Lyons do that brings out Mrs Johnstone's superstition?

6 What surprising news does Mrs Johnstone receive from the Gynaecologist?

7 How does Mrs Lyons plan to fool people into thinking that she has had a baby?

8 How do we know that Mrs Lyons is desperate to have a child?

9 What does Mrs Lyons believe all women suffer from in pregnancy?

10 Why does the Narrator say that 'there's no going back, for anyone'?

11 Mrs Johnstone remembers the removal of their table while they were eating their tea with a 'wry laugh'. What does 'wry' suggest about Mrs Johnstone's laugh?

12 Why is it urgent for Mrs Lyons that Mrs Johnstone hands over one of the twins?

13 What does Mrs Lyons stop Mrs Johnstone from doing when the baby is about to cry?

14 What excuse does Mrs Lyons give for sacking Mrs Lyons?

15 How does Mrs Lyons use superstition to terrify Mrs Johnstone into giving up her rights to the twin?

16 What might the Narrator mean when he says that 'the devil's got your number'?

17 In what ways are Mrs Lyons and Mrs Johnstone similar?

18 How is Mrs Lyons able to persuade Mrs Johnstone to give her a baby?

19 Why does Mrs Johnstone say 'that nothing's yours/On easy terms'?

20 To what extent could Mrs Johnstone be described as a 'victim'? Write a paragraph explaining your thoughts.

'Blood brothers'

Summary

It is seven years later. Mickey is playing 'mounted police an' Indians' with a toy gun. Mrs Johnstone warns Mickey not to play near the 'big houses in the park'. Mickey wishes that he was as old as Sammy and that he is 'nearly eight' years old, not seven as his mother thinks. Mickey meets Edward who approaches him as he has seen him playing near his house. Edward shocks Mickey by offering sweets without wanting anything in return. Mickey contrasts this behaviour with his older brother's behaviour who would have 'weed on' the sweets first. Mickey renames Edward as 'Eddie'. Edward admires Mickey's swearing and Mickey teaches him a new word. They pledge themselves as best friends and they become 'blood brothers' in a ritual where they promise to defend each other. (Here we see the motif of toy guns representing the violence that will appear throughout the play until it ends by shattering Mickey and Eddie's lives. As we have seen earlier, the stage directions give us clues to Willy Russell's intentions. In this case, Russell tells us in a stage direction that Mickey is *'fed up'* and *'somehow the magic has gone out of genocide'*. Although this is a joke here, Russell is pointing out that this imaginary violence can escalate into bigger and more serious forms of violence.)

We have already seen the differences between the lives of the Johnstone family and the Lyons family. Once again, Russell points out how something as simple of knocking on a door can make people in poverty anxious and fearful. Mrs Johnstone mistakes Mickey's knocking for the rent man. The suggestion here is that she owes money and doesn't have the means to pay it. The fact that Mickey – aged seven – understands this, shows the difference between his life and Eddie's more privileged life.

Look at the student's notes for a paragraph to answer the question:

What differences does Russell reveal between Mickey's life and Edward's life in the scene with Edward's sweets? Why does he do this?

Eddie = comfortable and generous

Mickey = suspicious and careful

Mickey sees generosity as 'soft'. Sammy = vindictive and bullying

Use these notes to write a paragraph of your own.

STRETCH IT!

Mickey explains to Edward that Sammy has a 'plate in his head' because he was dropped on his head and this is why he is 'dead mean sometimes'. Why do you think Russell includes this detail?

Rituals and rites of passage

Novels, films and plays often focus on **rites of passage**. These are events or experiences that mark important stages in life, such as birth, childhood to adulthood, marriage and death.

In this section, the audience sees Mickey wanting to be older – especially as old as his brother Sammy. This is a theme that recurs throughout the play, but sadly for Mickey, his adult life is nothing as he expected as a child.

The ritual that Mickey and Eddie perform to become 'blood brothers' is often associated with gang culture. A 'blood brother' can be a male blood relative or men who have sworn loyalty to each another. In this ritual, blood is mingled to seal the oath. In the play, Edward and Mickey cut a 'nick' (a small cut) in their hand before clamping their hands together. It is ironic that they are linked by their family blood as well as through this ritual. Notice the oath they pledge:

> **EDWARD**: I will always defend my brother…
> **MICKEY**: And stand by him.
> **EDWARD**: And stand by him.
> **MICKEY**: An' share all my sweets with him.
> **EDWARD**: And share…

Even here, Russell hints to the audience that because of their different class backgrounds, Mickey is naturally more closed and suspicious while Edward is able to be more generous and trusting.

DO IT!

1 During the oath, Mickey and Edward pledge to 'share' their sweets. Significantly, Edward doesn't complete his pledge as he is cut off by Sammy's entrance. What else do they share – or not share – during the play?

2 Mickey *'recites'* about Sammy's behaviour and how he wants to be older like Sammy. Russell shows the audience how Sammy's behaviour **foreshadows** his later actions in the play. Think about how the quotations below show this. The first one has been done for you.

'He's got two worms and a catapult' Sammy's love of weapons began when he was young. This led to his use of guns in a robbery and the deaths at the end of the play. 'He robbed me toy car y' know'

'He wees straight through the letter box'

What Edward learned

Summary

Sammy appears in front of Mickey and Edward with a gun in his hand. He immediately begins bullying the boys for sweets. He brags about getting an airgun rather than a cap gun. Sammy leaves the boys, who he labels as 'soft', to bury his worms. Mrs Johnstone meets Edward, banning him from going to play there again telling him that the 'bogey man' will get him. Edward reaches his home where his father gives him a toy gun and he asks his mother what the 'bogey man' is. Mickey appears at the door and asks if Edward can play. Mrs Lyons recognises him and sends him away. In his anger, Edward uses the language Mickey has taught him, as he calls her a 'fuckoff'. (Once again we see toy guns being used to foreshadow the violence that will erupt later in the play. In this section, Russell shows the audience how the toys become ever more powerful and real, in this case Sammy's desire for an air rifle. Although an air pistol wouldn't usually kill people, it is a dangerous firearm and can inflict a nasty wound. From the air pistol he will move onto other guns of course. This motif continues as Mr Lyons presents Edward with a toy gun. Mr Lyons pretends to die when Edward aims it at him. However as the audience knows from the opening scene, it is Edward and Mickey who will die. This episode has structural significance.)

Twin bonds

Edward and Mickey are instantly drawn to each other when they meet, despite Edward being a 'poshy'. Russell is suggesting that their blood bond as brothers means that they will naturally be drawn to each other. Ironically, Mickey tries to defend Edward against Sammy's bullying, showing his loyalty towards Edward in the face of his other brotherly tie with Sammy.

The differences between the boys are shown through the way Russell uses **language** in their dialogue. Edward refers to his mother as 'mummy' whereas Mickey refers to his mother as 'mam'; this colloquialism indicating their class differences. Edward's middle-class upbringing is also shown by his use of the middle-class slang, 'smashing', and by how no one in his family shortens his name. It is significant that it is Mickey who re-names him as 'Eddie'. The name links Edward to the working classes yet also the ritual of naming strengthens the bond between Edward and Mickey.

STRETCH IT!

Why do you think Russell includes the detail of Sammy killing the worms? Write a paragraph explaining what it tells us about Sammy.

Look at the list of **characteristics** below. Which do you think describe Mickey and which describe Edward? Write a brief explanation of your choices.

suspicious	trusting	generous	admiring
protective	streetwise	enlightening	innocent

The two mothers

Summary

In this section, as seen previously in the play, Willy Russell uses **structure** to show the parallels between the lives of Edward and Mickey as well as showing the differences in their lives because of class differences.

After telling Edward not to 'come round here again', we see Mrs Johnstone singing a lament showing her suffering as she realises what she has lost through the deal. She sings that the deal and their relationship will be 'concealed', suggesting that it will be covered up to deceive the world. The audience knows that this will bring **tragedy** as they have witnessed this in the play's opening scene. (See page 82 for further information about tragedy.)

Like Mrs Johnstone, Mrs Lyons recognises Mickey when he appears at her house to play with Edward. By trying to separate the two friends, she causes an outburst from Edward where he uses the new 'smashing' word from Mickey as he calls her a 'fuckoff'. Russell uses this language to shock as he shows Mickey's influence over Edward that triggers an equally shocking action from Mrs Lyons as she 'hits EDWARD *hard and instinctively.'* Russell illustrates that violence doesn't just exist in the lives and homes of the working classes, but it also exists in middle-class homes too. Her following outburst reveals how possessive she is as she realises that Edward is looking at her in *'terror'*.

AQA exam-style question

To what extent does the audience feel sympathy towards Mrs Lyons in *Blood Brothers?*

Write about:

- how Mrs Lyons presents Mrs Lyons' actions and behaviour
- how Russell presents Mrs Lyons by the way he writes.

[30 marks]

DO IT!

Here is a student's plan for this question. Can you write another two bullet points?

- overarching idea - Mrs Lyons manipulates Mrs Johnstone when she makes up the superstition of the twins dying but by the end of the play her deception and the superstition become truth, causing her downfall.
- At the start of the play, Mrs Lyons is seen sympathetically as she is lonely and childless in her 'pretty house' but very quickly the audience sees the lengths she will go to to have a child.
- Mrs Lyons manipulates Mrs Johnstone by preying on her superstitious nature and making false promises. She sacks Mrs Johnstone callously to cut her out of Edward's life. At this point, the audience does not have sympathy for her.

It's just a game

Summary

The scene begins with Edward sitting alone in his garden as children from the Johnstone's neighbourhood play a series of violent games, from *'cowboys and Indians',* to gangsters, to war games. Sammy is on one team and Mickey and Linda are together on another team. The children repeat that 'the whole thing's just a game' so there will be no consequences. In a confrontation with Sammy, Mickey tells him to 'fuck off'. The children say Mickey will die because of this. Upset, Mickey tells Linda he is afraid of dying. Mickey and Linda go to find Edward. Showing him Sammy's air pistol, they tempt him to go to the park with them to shoot the statue of Peter Pan. Edward is worried about the police, but Linda and Mickey impress him by saying how they respond to policemen. Mickey, Linda and Edward leave as Mrs Lyons calls for Edward. The Narrator enters singing about stolen babies and fate. (Notice how the Narrator mentions stories about stolen babies. He uses the words that he used to Mrs Johnstone that 'the devil's got your number'. The time is running out for her secret and her security.)

Children's games and contemporary references

In this scene, the violence in the games has escalated. The children sing that 'if you cross your fingers/And if you count from one to ten/You can get up off the ground again'. Unfortunately for Mickey and Edward, and of course the rest of society, however much they 'cross their fingers', they will still die at the end of the play. In all of these scenes, the children show events based on television programmes that audiences, especially in the 1960s–1980s, would be familiar with.

Al Capone	An American criminal gang leader in the 1920s and 1930s. One of his activities was making and selling alcohol – illegal at this time in America because of Prohibition.
Elliot Ness	Lead a team to enforce Prohibition in 1930s America. His team, known as The Untouchables, was tasked with bringing down Al Capone.
Cowboy	Cowboy films often contained a dramatic scene with a gun fight where two cowboys face each other across a street. The 'fastest draw' won the battle. These films were popular throughout the time in which the play is set.
Ninth Brigade	War films re-emerged in the 1980s, often depicting American war scenes and featuring a 'hotshot' sergeant who would be tough on his troops but had a heart of gold.
Professor Howe	Scientists created the atom bomb which was perceived as a continuous threat to society. This fear reached a height in the 1970s and 1980s.

DO IT!

Note how the children's games become increasingly violent. Write a paragraph to explain why Willy Russell includes these scenes. What do you think he might be suggesting about the influence of television and film on children?

Linda and Mickey

Again we see a superstition in action as it impacts on Mickey. The other children tell him that he will die for swearing. Linda immediately comes to his aid. In the stage directions she *'moves in to protect* MICKEY*'*, immediately turning on the children to support the *'visibly shaken'* Mickey. From this point she takes on the threatening Sammy as she approaches *'undaunted'* to warn him:

> **LINDA**: I'll tell my mother why all her ciggies always disappear when you're in our house.

Linda is shrewd and unafraid. She understands the way Sammy behaves and is not afraid to confront him about it. Notice how Sammy does not retaliate. Instead, he moves away. Russell is pointing out that Sammy, the bully is, of course, a coward underneath his confident swagger.

Mickey confesses that he fears death. Linda once again protects him by comforting him, telling him that he will meet his 'twinny again' when he dies. Linda is protective and fearless in her support of Mickey. This support is the kind of support that we would expect a mother to give. Although Mrs Johnstone loves her son, she is unable to protect him in the direct way that Linda does. This is a pattern that Russell uses throughout the play.

Despite the role of protector, Linda is also a mischief-maker. Here we see her immediately introducing Edward to the air pistol, telling him that they 'try an' shoot' the statue of Peter Pan's 'little thingy off'. She also joins in the cheek given to the policemen, which so greatly impresses Edward. (Peter Pan is a fictional character from the novel by J.M. Barrie. He lives perpetually as a young boy as he never grows up. He symbolises childhood mischief and innocence.)

DO IT!

Look at this extract from the scene.

> **MICKEY**: We say dead funny things to them, don't we, Linda?
> **EDWARD**: What sort of funny things?
> **LINDA**: All sorts, don't we Mickey?
> **MICKEY**: Yeh…like y' know when they ask what y' name is, we say things like, like 'Adolf Hitler', don't we Linda?
> **LINDA**: Yeh, an' hey Eddie, y' know when they say, 'What d' y' think you're doin'?' we always say somethin' like like, 'waitin' for the ninety-two bus'.
> **EDWARD** (*greatly impressed*): Do you…do you really? Goodness that's fantastic.

What do you think Willy Russell's language choices in this scene show us about the three characters? Write five bullet points to show your ideas. You might want to consider the effects of aspects such as Standard English, colloquialism, **dialect**, stage directions, noun choices, formality, sentence types.

Character and theme essentials

Superstition

Mrs Johnstone threatens Edward with the 'bogey man' – a supernatural creature that will punish misbehaving children. It is her first thought when faced with a difficult situation. Mrs Lyons explains away the 'bogey man' as a '…superstition. The sort of thing a silly mother might say to her children'. Although Mrs Lyons presents the rational line of argument when faced by superstition, she used her false superstition to persuade Mrs Johnstone to stay away from Edward.

Within the children's games we see superstition used when it is suggested that the deaths that occur in their fantasy games can be put right if 'you cross your fingers/And you count to ten'. Throughout the play, the casual attitude towards violence hints that the superstition of crossed fingers will protect the characters. However, at the end of the play, Russell shows the audience that the violence is real and therefore more shocking.

Hopes and dreams

As a seven-year-old Mickey says that 'I wish I was our Sammy' when he tells the audience of his wish to be older and more grown up. This desire to be older recurs throughout the play – unfortunately for Mickey, his adult life does not match his seven-year-old dreams.

Mrs Johnstone

Willy Russell demonstrates us the impact of poverty on Mrs Johnstone as he shows her reaction to Mickey knocking insistently at the door. She is depicted *'screaming'* as she believes the knock is coming from one of her many debt collectors, then responds *'with relief'* when she realises it is Mickey. She warns Mickey to stay away from Edward because she is afraid of Mrs Lyon's made-up superstition but is *'stunned'* when Mickey introduces Edward as his 'blood brother'. She orders Edward away from the house with the threat of the 'bogey man', again showing her dependence on superstition.

Mrs Lyons

Mrs Lyons' worries about her secret being discovered reach a climax when Edward tells her that he and Mickey are 'blood brothers' when Mickey comes to call for him to play. Her protectiveness boils over with rage and frustration leading her to lash out, violently hitting him *'hard and instinctively.'* She loves her son, but wants to have that love to herself. Notice how she draws Edward away to read a story with her after he plays boisterously with his father. Edward's *'delighted'* reaction to his father's play shows how unusual this is in the Lyons' household. Her prejudices regarding the working classes (and of course the Johnstone family) are shown when she tells Edward that he must stay away from 'boys like that'. She goes on to tell Edward that he will 'learn filth from them' and that he is 'not like them'. This is, of course, ironic as he really is just like them despite her protestations that he is 'my son, mine'.

REVIEW IT!

1 Who does Mickey suggest his mother fears might be at the door when he tries to get into the house?

2 What reason does Mrs Johnstone give to Mickey to explain why Sammy always steals his things?

3 When Mickey tells his mother that in play they 'wiped out three thousand Indians', how does she respond?

4 In the verse 'I wish I was our Sammy,' what does Sammy do to Mickey's toy car?

5 Why is Mickey suspicious when Edward offers him a sweet?

6 What happens to Sammy's worms?

7 What name does Mickey give Edward? Why is this important?

8 What **adjective** does Mrs Lyons use to describe mothers who threaten their children with the bogey man?

9 Who says, 'I like him more than you'? Why is this significant?

10 Linda says, 'I stopped it with the bin lid'. Who does she say it to and why?

11 Who plays Professor Howe in the children's games scene? What is he carrying?

12 What do the children say will happen if you swear?

13 What action do you need to do to escape death according to the children?

14 When Mickey says he is scared of death, Linda dries his tears. Why do you think Russell includes this stage direction?

15 What possession of Sammy's does Mickey have?

16 When Mickey and Linda go to see Edward, what is the first thing he tells them?

17 How many times does Linda say that a policeman has caught her and Mickey?

18 How does Edward react to their tales of how they behave towards the police?

19 The Narrator repeats song lyrics as a warning to Mrs Lyons. What are these lyrics and what do they suggest?

20 What clues are we given in this section that Sammy will grow up to be a bad character?

Act One:
Moving and goodbye

Serious crime or prank?

Summary

Mrs Lyons tries to persuade her husband that they should move away to keep Edward safe. He is irritated that she has called him home from work and suggests that she needs to see a doctor for her nerves. (Mr Lyons' language suggests he has no real sympathy or patience with his wife: 'For Christ's sake…'; 'Oh Christ'.)

Mr Lyons picks up a pair of Edward's shoes and puts them on the table. She sweeps them off in superstitious terror. In a song, the Narrator now warns her that the devil's got her number and will find her. (Note how the Narrator gives the same warning to Mrs Lyons that he earlier gave to Mrs Johnstone. This suggests they are equally guilty in the 'sale' of baby Edward.)

Meanwhile, Mickey, Linda and Edward are taking it in turns to fire the air pistol at a target. When Mickey keeps missing and Linda keeps hitting, Mickey refuses to play anymore. Linda suggests they throw stones through some windows. They are just about to do it when a policeman arrives. To the horror of the other two children, Edward laughs as he tells the Policeman they are 'waiting for the ninety-two bus' and that his name is 'Adolph Hitler'. When he realises that the others aren't laughing, he starts crying and the Policeman leads them away.

DO IT!

Read the Policeman's speech beginning 'An' er, as I say'. Why is this speech important? Make notes on what the Policeman says and does.

STRETCH IT!

Look carefully at the *way* the Policeman speaks. What might Willy Russell want us to notice, and to learn from this?

The Policeman warns Mrs Johnstone that Mickey was 'about to commit a serious crime' and that she will 'end up in court again'. Then he reassures the Lyons that what Edward was about to do was nothing more than 'a prank', and has a friendly drink with them before leaving. (As a representative of authority, the Policeman treats Mickey and Edward differently for the same 'crime'. He is prejudiced against working-class Mickey, and tolerant towards middle-class Edward.)

'The devil's got your number'

> MRS LYONS: ...we have got to move, Richard. Because if we stay here I feel that something terrible will happen, something bad.
>
> MR LYONS: Look, Jen. What is this thing you keep talking about getting away from?

Mrs Lyons feels as though something is closing in on her and she dreads it. Perhaps it is her guilty conscience. We do know that in literal terms the thing that is hunting her down is the risk that Edward's real identity will be revealed. The fact that she 'keeps' talking about her fear shows that it is getting stronger.

> NARRATOR: Now you know the devil's got your number
> He's gonna find y'
> He's starin' through your windows
> He's creeping down the hall.

The Narrator warns Mrs Lyons here with the same words he earlier used to warn Mrs Johnstone. The Narrator's words are sinister. You can almost feel Mrs Lyon's past 'crime' coming back to haunt her. The images of the 'devil' spying on her through windows and 'creeping down the hall' connect the Narrator's warning to tense scenes in horror films.

Blood mothers?

Just as Eddie and Mickey are joined as 'blood brothers', the two mothers are joined in the terrible secret that they bought and sold a baby. The women are also like twins, and the identical language implies that they are identical in important ways.

NAILIT!

In your AQA exam, it is very important to prepare to answer the question carefully. Highlight the key words in the question. What are they asking you to do? (See page 84.)

AQA exam-style question

'You get the feeling that both Mrs Johnstone and Mrs Lyons feel hunted and trapped.'

How far do you agree with this view of the two women?

Write about:

- what the two women say and do and what others say about them in the play

- how Russell presents the situation the two women are in by the ways he writes.

[30 marks]

DOIT!

Copy out the question above and annotate it (make notes around it) to make sure you understand exactly what is required.

The locket

Summary

Mr Lyons tells Edward that for the sake of his mother's health they should move nearer the countryside. Edward doesn't want to move, but he visits the Johnstones to tell them he is going.

Mrs Johnstone answers the door and when Edward tells her he doesn't want to move and will miss his friend Mickey, she cuddles him to comfort him. Edward asks her to buy a house near to the Lyons' new house. (Mrs Johnstone is amused by Edward's naivety: he doesn't realise that other people are not as fortunate as his own family, and cannot just buy new houses when they want to.)

Mrs Johnstone gives Edward a locket as a memento. It contains a picture of Mrs Johnstone and Mickey when he was much younger. Edward is very pleased. Mrs Johnstone tells him to keep it a secret. (The locket secret is another example of a pact. Again, this will have dangerous consequences that neither partner to the pact predicts.)

Edward calls Mrs Johnstone 'smashing'. Mickey comes out to say goodbye and Edward gives him a parting gift of a toy gun. (As the two boys part they 'clasp hands', reminding us of the blood bond they made earlier. Guns are a recurring motif, and the gift of a gun here reinforces their bond, but ironically, it is a gun that destroys the bond at the end of the play.)

Secrets

A number of secrets are important in **Act** One, and all of them threaten eventual disaster. The secrets include:

- Mrs Lyons' lies to her husband about 'their baby'
- Mrs Lyons' and Mrs Johnstone's secret deal over Edward
- Mickey's 'borrowing' of his brother's airgun
- Mrs Johnstone's gift to Edward of the locket.

DO IT!

Use the table to explore some secrets in Act One; how they are introduced and their significance.
Some ideas have been given to start you off.

Secret	How it is introduced	Significance
The 'borrowing' of the airgun	Mickey produces the gun with a smile, showing that he doesn't realise the significance of guns despite the kids' play-killing just before. The audience will feel apprehensive.	This airgun is a stepping stone to the real gun Mickey also finds and uses at the end.
The locket		

Avoiding the truth

Here Mr Lyons talks to his son in a light and jokey way that does not signal how important this move is. He seems to be seeking his son's approval, but when Edward firmly rejects the proposal, Mr Lyons' choice of words suggests that the proposal is still up for negotiation: he starts with the word 'well' which implies that Mr Lyons is not fully decided, and calling Edward 'old chap' – a term he might use to address work colleagues – makes it sound as though Edward has an equal say in the decision. Typically, Mr Lyons is avoiding a difficult issue.

> **MR LYONS**: …Do you think you'd like that?
> **EDWARD**: I want to stay here.
> **MR LYONS**: Well, you think about it, old chap.

Like Mr Lyons, Mrs Johnstone does not address Edward's fears and desires truthfully: instead she tries to soothe him with her prediction that he will love his new home, even though she does not offer any reason why that might be true. The fact that she stops after 'listen', pauses and then repeats the word hints that she might have been about to say something else, and disguises her intention.

> **EDWARD** (*through his tears*): I don't want to go. I want to stay here where my friends are… where Mickey is.
> **MRS JOHNSTONE**: Come here.
> *She takes him, cradling him, letting him cry.*
> No listen…listen, don't you be soft. You'll probably love it in your new house.

DO IT!

Write a paragraph explaining the main differences (or similarities) between how Mr Lyons and Mrs Johnstone respond to Edward's unwillingness to move.

Mother–son bond

'*Cradling*' Edward and '*letting him cry*' – implying that she almost encourages it – puts Mrs Johnstone in a motherly role. She is making up for the time when Mrs Lyons prevented her from taking Edward out of his cradle and comforting him when he was about to cry. The audience will notice the significance of this: Mrs Johnstone is unconsciously re-asserting her maternal rights, and Edward senses the bond between them. The locket gift symbolises this re-bonding.

STRETCH IT!

How is this 'goodbye' scene relevant to the theme of secrets and lies? What does it add to the theme of secrets and lies within families?

'Oh, bright new day'

Summary

Edward shows no enthusiasm for his new home. Mr Lyons reassures his wife that Edward will settle naturally very soon. (Once again Mr Lyons just hopes that a problem will pass: he offers no solution and it seems as though he thinks any problems are only in his wife's mind.)

Mickey feels lost and lonely without Edward. He recalls all of Edward's qualities – generosity, knowledge and tidiness. Edward misses Mickey just as much but for quite different virtues: swearing, humour, untidiness and being active and adventurous. (Russell gives Mickey a song verse praising his brother's qualities and has them both sing the last **phrase** – 'my friend' – together. Then they sing 'my friend' together at the end of Edward's verse praising Mickey. This song structure symbolises their unity, but also makes their separation all the sadder for the audience.)

Mrs Johnstone is delighted to hear that the family are being rehoused in a better, cleaner area, so that they can make a new start. Her neighbours predict a drop in crime and nuisance in the area. (Mrs Johnstone's exaggerated expectations of their new home – vast garden, air so pure it makes you 'drunk' – show her deep and surprising optimism. Her dreams of happiness always end up in the image of dancing.)

As soon as they arrive in their new neighbourhood, the Johnstone children start misbehaving and Mrs Johnstone has to tell Sammy to get off a cow that turns out to be a bull.

The twins

Read how one student makes a point about how Russell presents the twins, and strengthens the point by referring to details. Notice how they use indirect reference *and* quotation.

> Willy Russell presents Edward and Mickey as opposites: for example, one is clean, the other is dirty. However, Russell also presents the brothers as equals. This is suggested by giving each brother a verse with an identical structure, and a shared ending: identical structure for twins who are 'as like...as two new pins'. The structure and content of their verses makes them seem like two halves of one whole person.

DO IT!

Write a few more lines about how Russell presents the relationship between the twins in this scene. Refer to the text to support your ideas.

Mrs Johnstone's dream of a better life

> **MRS JOHNSTONE** (*singing*): Oh, bright new day,
> We're movin' away.
> **MICKEY** (*speaking*): Mam? What's up?
> **MRS JOHNSTONE** (*singing*): We're startin' all over again.

The close rhymes give Mrs Johnstone's words a childish simplicity that expresses her simple delight.

Mrs Johnstone is delighted by the chance of a new start. Her dream is always to escape her mistakes and misfortunes, and not have her life defined by the past.

'Destination' reminds us of 'destiny' – fate. Mrs Johnstone looks forward to a different future where she can build a different 'reputation' – a better version of herself. She wants to escape the prison that has been created by past events. The quickly repeated '-ation' rhyme helps to suggest her breathless excitement.

> **MRS JOHNSTONE** (*singing*):
> Got a new situation,
> A new destination,
> And no reputation following me.

> **MRS JOHNSTONE** (*singing*):
> Now that we're movin'
> Now that we're improvin',
> Let's just wash our hands of this lot.

The **metaphor**, 'Wash our hands of', is a cliché, but it does express the importance for Mrs Johnstone of getting rid of the evidence of past problems and failures. A happy new life depends on escaping from their old life – and other people's negative perceptions of the family.

AQA exam-style question

How does Willy Russell present the power of hopes and desires in *Blood Brothers*?

Write about:

- the hopes and desires of some characters

- how Russell presents these hopes and desires by the way he writes.

[30 marks]

Here is a student's rough outline plan for an answer that includes four main points.

1. What Mrs Johnstone wanted, and what she wants after her husband leaves her.

2. Mrs Johnstone's admirable optimism and defiance - refusal to give in to harsh reality.

3. What Mrs Lyons wants and how Russell makes us feel about it.

4. The effect that these hopes and desires have on the characters and the plot - positive and destructive (Sammy?)

DOIT!

Set a timer for three minutes.

On a large piece of paper, draw a spider diagram of everything you can remember about different characters' hopes and desires. Choose three or four characters. Spend three minutes for each character. Mark links between different characters' hopes and desires.

Character and theme essentials

Social class

Because Edward comes from a wealthier household, he is treated more leniently by the police than Mickey. The sort of social prejudice shown by the Policeman is one of the reasons that Mrs Johnstone cannot escape her 'fate': she is trapped by prejudice. Even during the first act, Russell makes it clear to the audience that what might look like the workings of fate are actually the workings of the class system.

Fate and superstition

When Mrs Lyons is terrified about her husband putting shoes on the table, she seems to have caught Mrs Johnstone's superstition. In fact, Russell is really suggesting that what we secretly do in the past will always catch up with us eventually: as the Narrator says, debts have to be paid. Fate – or the 'devil' – is always 'right behind y", watching and waiting.

Hopes and dreams

Mrs Johnstone is old before her time, worn out and worn down, but she never stops dreaming of a better life. When she hears that the family is being rehoused, her optimism revives immediately. 'I haven't seen you happy like this for ages,' says Mickey. Although she is depressed by her conditions, Mrs Johnstone never really accepts that poverty is her unalterable fate. The extravagance of her dreams – for example, the Pope coming round for tea – expresses her basic belief in the possibility of escape to a 'bright new day'.

Mrs Johnstone

Despite the grinding poverty that Mrs Johnstone has to cope with and her conflict with the law, Mrs Johnstone is remarkably self-controlled, optimistic and selfless, always putting others' needs above her own. When her lost son, Edward, comes to say goodbye for ever, Mrs Johnstone responds with dignity and affection, giving him the locket as a reminder of her and Mickey. Although she must expect never to see him again, she wishes him well, comforts him and reassures him that he will be happy in his new home. In many ways she is resigned to the circumstances of her life, but when the chance of a new life arrives, her excitement and optimism resurfaces. Russell is perhaps presenting Mrs Johnstone as a model of working-class resilience.

Mr Lyons

Mr Lyons shows formal concern for his wife, but really he does not want anything to disrupt his working life, which he puts above his family life. His wife's 'nerves' are an inconvenience to him and he always looks for solutions that will trouble him as little as possible. For many readers (or viewers) Mr Lyons' lukewarm sympathy for his wife will probably evoke sympathy for Mrs Lyons and perhaps show him as an example of male dominance.

Edward

Edward is naive. He doesn't recognise the difference between bravado and bravery, so he takes Linda and Mickey's advice about handling policemen as literal, and makes a dangerous fool of himself. He also has no understanding of why the Johnstones cannot just buy a new house: he assumes everyone shares his own economic advantages. Edward's innocence is part of his appeal.

Linda

At this point in the play Linda is the mischief leader, daring Mickey and Edward to join her in throwing stones at windows, taunting Edward with being 'scared'. She is a much better shot with the airgun than Mickey is.

REVIEW IT!

1 What does Mrs Lyons try to persuade her husband to agree to when she is worrying about where Edward has gone?

2 How does Mr Lyons frighten his wife?

3 Why does Mickey end the children's game with the airgun?

4 What name does Edward give to the Policeman?

5 What suggests that the Policeman is treating Edward's behaviour lightly?

6 What surprises Mrs Johnstone when she answers the door to Edward?

7 Why does Mrs Johnstone call herself and Edward 'a right pair'?

8 What is in the locket that Mrs Johnstone gives Edward?

9 What does Edward do with the locket?

10 When Mrs Lyons worries about Edward's unhappiness in their new home, what advice does Mr Lyons give her?

11 Why does Mickey visit Edward's old home?

12 What news excites Mrs Johnstone?

13 For what reason does Sammy think Mrs Johnstone has called him?

14 Why are the neighbours pleased that the Johnstones are leaving?

15 In their new home, what does Mrs Johnstone hope will happen at the weekends?

16 Why does Mrs Johnstone see moving as leading to a 'bright new day'?

17 Why is Mr Lyons frustrated with Mrs Lyons?

18 When Edward puts on the locket, why does he look at Mrs Johnstone 'a moment too long'?

19 In what ways does Willy Russell show that Mrs Johnstone is very excited to be rehoused?

20 At the end of Act One, should an audience share Mrs Johnstone's optimism?

Act Two: *The deal*

Suspended

Summary

Seven years later, Mrs Johnstone is happy in her new home where the neighbours never fight in the week and the Milkman takes her dancing, telling her that she has legs like Marilyn Monroe, a famous, glamorous but tragic actor of that time. (Notice that once again, we have a gap of seven years. In fairy tales and superstitions, seven is known as a magic number.)

The audience learn that Sammy burnt down the school, but Mrs Johnstone thinks that it is the fault of the school for letting him play with 'magnesium'. The judge in Sammy's court case is lenient and thinks that she had legs like Marilyn Monroe and wants to take her dancing. Mrs Johnstone tells the audience that Mickey is growing up and is becoming interested in girls. (Once again in this section Russell links Mrs Johnstone to the beautiful but ultimately tragic Marilyn Monroe.)

Mrs Lyons is teaching Edward to ballroom dance before he returns to boarding school. Mr Lyons sounds the car horn to let Edward know that they need to leave. In a parallel scene, Mrs Johnstone is *'hustling'* Mickey to school while teasing him about Linda. Sammy heads out to sign on to 'the dole'. The Narrator enters as the Conductor, asking Mrs Johnstone if she is happy. He ominously goes on to ask her if she has forgotten the past. Sammy tries to get onto the bus with a child's fare. The Conductor refuses to let him have a ticket at that rate and Sammy threatens him with a knife. (Like the events that have moved on in the play, so has the danger associated with Sammy's weapons. He has moved on from the toy gun and airgun to a knife. This will soon become a real gun.)

Linda and Mickey get off the bus and Linda tells Mickey that she hopes that he doesn't ever 'do anything soft' like Sammy. She tells him that she loves him but Mickey hurries off.

Edward gets into a confrontation about his locket with a teacher as he refuses to take it off and he is suspended. In a parallel scene, Mickey and Linda are in a geography class. Mickey gets into a confrontation with the teacher; Linda rises to his defence, which results in them both being suspended.

DEFINE IT!

the dole
– claiming unemployment benefit; people had to attend the Benefits office to sign that they were available for work

DO IT!

In this section, both Linda and Mickey are shown by Russell to be growing up. How do their attitudes towards love and the opposite sex differ?

The Narrator and fate

In this section the Narrator appears as the conductor of the bus that Mickey, Linda and Sammy catch. Seeing Mrs Johnstone, he speaks directly to her:

Until this point, the audience has felt hopeful in the new life that the Johnstone family have found. Even Sammy, having burnt down the school, was dealt with lightly. The Conductor's questions shatter the happy picture that has been painted.

The Narrator as the Conductor gives voice to fate as he ominously reminds Mrs Johnstone that she has things in her past that she has tried to forget.

" **CONDUCTOR** (*speaking*): Happy are y'. Content at last?
Wiped out what happened, forgotten the past?
She looks at him, puzzled
But you've got to have an endin' if a start's been made.
No one gets off without the price being paid "

The Narrator foretells that Mrs Johnstone will get what she deserves for her past actions. In fairy tales, everyone has to pay their part of a deal or a pact.

DO IT!

In parallel scenes, Russell shows us life in school for Edward and Mickey. Despite the very different establishments, the outcome is the same for both boys as they are suspended from school.

Complete the table below to help you analyse the parallels between these scenes. Some boxes have been filled in to help you.

Parallels between scenes	Edward	Mickey
What the audience learns about Edward and Mickey's future prospects		Mickey is asked 'how the hell do you hope to find a job'. The teacher implies he is destined to be unemployed.
How the teacher speaks to Edward and Mickey at the start of the confrontation	The teacher 'looks down his nose' at Edward and tells him that he is 'rather big for [his] boots', suggesting that he is arrogant.	
The 'offence' committed by Edward and Mickey		Mickey isn't listening in class and is unable to respond to the teacher's question.

How Edward and Mickey react to the teacher	Edward refuses to hand over the locket before using the "F" word that Mickey taught him in response to the teacher's threat. This shows that Edward and Mickey are close in temperament and thinking.	

'There's a woman gone mad'

Summary

Mrs Lyons is reading the letter detailing Edward's suspension. She asks to see the locket, believing that it is a present from a girlfriend. Edward won't tell her where he got it because it is a 'secret'. Mrs Lyons opens it, only to see to her horror that it's a picture of Mrs Johnstone and Mickey who she mistakes for Edward. (Notice the return to the theme of secrets. Edward exits with, 'everybody has secrets, don't you have secrets?': the audience knows that Mrs Lyons has many secrets.)

The Narrator returns to remind Mrs Lyons that her past actions will catch up with her. (Here we have a parallel with the Narrator's remarks to Mrs Johnstone in the role of the Conductor.)

Mickey and Linda are making their way up a hill. They notice someone looking out of a window. To tease Mickey, Linda says how 'gorgeous' the boy is. When Mickey does not seem to be jealous, she leaves. Only then can Mickey say how he feels about her. The boy in the window is Edward.

In a song, Edward and Mickey show how they each envy the other. They meet and Mickey asks Edward for a cigarette who says he will get some. They recognise each other and are joyfully reunited. (This is a parallel scene to where the boys shared sweets in Act One.)

Edward and Mickey discuss girlfriends and Mickey finally admits that he hasn't yet asked Linda out. Edward offers advice. The boys go to the Johnstone house for Mickey to borrow money to go to the cinema to see a 'racy' film to 'see how it's done'. Edward shows Mrs Johnstone that he still wears the locket. Edward and Mickey attempt to lie about the content of the film, but Mrs Johnstone catches them out good-naturedly. Mrs Lyons has followed the boys and appears in Mrs Johnstone's kitchen. Mrs Lyons offers money for Mrs Johnstone to move away, which she refuses. Mrs Lyons takes a knife from the drawer and lunges at Mrs Johnstone who disarms her. Mrs Lyons curses Mrs Johnstone and exits to the chanting of children that 'there's a woman gone mad'. (Curses, where someone appeals to supernatural forces to cause harm, often feature in fairy tales.)

STRETCH IT!

Willy Russell implies that they boys look alike (for example, Mrs Lyons thinks that Mickey is Edward in the photograph) but doesn't ever say they are identical twins. Can you think of a practical reason why this might be?

DO IT!

Look at the song where Edward and Mickey duet beginning 'If I was like him'. What does this song reveal about the boys? How does this impact on their relationship later in the play? Write a paragraph to explain your ideas.

A confrontation between two mothers

In this section we see parallel scenes with Mrs Johnstone and Mrs Lyons as mothers. Willy Russell shows how motherhood can be nurturing and loving as well as destructive and stifling. In the confrontation between the two women where Mrs Lyons is 'a woman gone mad', Russell shows the audience how Mrs Lyons' insecurity about her hold over her son can spill out into irrational behaviour.

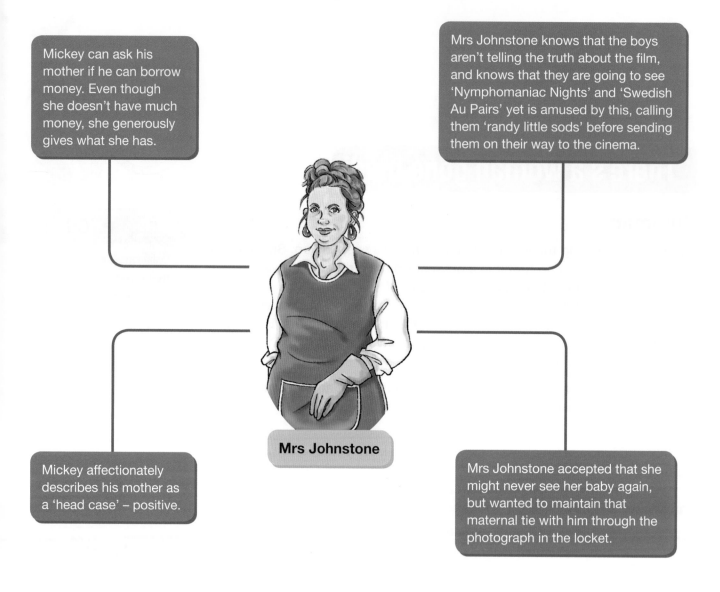

Mickey can ask his mother if he can borrow money. Even though she doesn't have much money, she generously gives what she has.

Mrs Johnstone knows that the boys aren't telling the truth about the film, and knows that they are going to see 'Nymphomaniac Nights' and 'Swedish Au Pairs' yet is amused by this, calling them 'randy little sods' before sending them on their way to the cinema.

Mrs Johnstone

Mickey affectionately describes his mother as a 'head case' – positive.

Mrs Johnstone accepted that she might never see her baby again, but wanted to maintain that maternal tie with him through the photograph in the locket.

Edward is unable to confide in his mother. He cannot tell her about the locket – a symbol of a maternal connection.

Mrs Lyons begins to follow and spy on her son in secret. She cannot ask him what he is doing because their relationship is not close enough for him to confide in her.

Mrs Lyons

Edward wants to avoid his mother seeing him. His reason for this is, 'She's off her beam, my Ma' – negative.

Mrs Lyons tells Mrs Johnstone that 'I took him. But I never made him mine.' Suggesting that like the gypsies mentioned by the Narrator, she stole the baby.

AQA exam-style question

How does Willy Russell present motherhood in *Blood Brothers*?

Write about:

- the way Mrs Johnstone and Mrs Lyons behave towards their children
- how Russell presents the two mothers by the way he writes.

[30 marks]

Here is a student's rough outline plan for an answer that includes four main points.

1. Overarching idea: the two mothers are like twins but represent opposites in their natures. Mrs Johnstone is loving and maternal. Mrs Lyons is cold and possessive.

2. Mrs Johnstone tries the best for her children, even to the point of giving one away, but is a victim of her poverty.

3. Mrs Lyons has money and possessions but does not have love from her husband and son - or the ability to love selflessly herself.

4. The effect that the two maternal natures have on the plot - positive and destructive elements.

DO IT!

Add another two bullet points to complete this plan. Develop the plan by finding evidence to support at least two of the points.

The three of them

Summary

Mickey and Edward emerge from the cinema and bump into Linda with a friend. They have also been to the cinema. The friend leaves and Linda asks what film they saw. Mickey and Edward speak at the same time with Mickey saying, untruthfully, 'Bridge over the River Kwai' and Edward almost revealing the truth. Linda, unabashed, tells them that she saw 'Nymphomaniac Nights'. (Both Edward and Mickey are embarrassed by their choice of film. Notice how Mickey lies in this situation while Linda is open and frank.) Edward is leaping and shouting, when a policeman approaches them. The three respond with the taunts they claimed to use when they were children. A further four years passes over the course of a song where snapshots of their friendship are shown. (Russell is using a summarising technique here that we would most often see used in films rather than in the theatre.)

Edward waits by a streetlamp as Linda approaches. She says that Mickey is working overtime. Edward explains that he is going to university the following day. He asks if he can write to her, that is, if Mickey wouldn't mind. Linda tells him that she is not Mickey's girlfriend – he hasn't asked her out. Edward sings about how he would behave within a relationship with Linda if he was 'the guy, if I/Was in his shoes' but says that he will not say 'a word'. (Edward loves Linda but his blood oath to Mickey is stronger. He would not betray him.) Mickey enters and Edward gets him to ask Linda out. (Not only does Edward not

tell Linda how he feels, he actively encourages Mickey to ask her out. Here we have the love triangle that will prove fatal at the end of the play.) Mickey does and Linda agrees with a quick, 'Yeh'. Mickey arranges to see Edward at Christmas and he offers to pay for a party. Edward agrees with, 'It's a deal'. They both thank Edward for getting them together and with their arms around each other, they watch Edward leave.

Dancing

Dancing is used by Willy Russell to represent the fleeting moments of happiness or pleasure that cannot last. Dancing can also represent nostalgia (looking back fondly to the past) and can be tinged with sadness. When you reach a moment of dance in the play, it is important to consider who is dancing and what happens directly afterwards.

DO IT!

In this scene, Edward grabs Linda's friend and dances with her before she escapes. What happens directly afterwards? What is Willy Russell pointing out to the audience?

Growing up

The Narrator appears as the rifle range man, who tells the audience about growing up and gives Linda a specific warning:

Lambs symbolise youth and innocence. The Narrator suggests that the innocence the three friends share will soon pass as the 'seasons' – and time – moves on.

> And who'd dare tell the lambs in Spring,
> What fate the later seasons bring.
> Who'd tell the girl in the middle of the pair
> The price she will pay for just being there

Like the other women in the play, Linda must 'pay the price' for her involvement with the two brothers. She will face the sorrow of the tragic events at the end of the play as a young mother.

Hopes and dreams

In this section, Edward reveals his feelings for Linda in a song. He sings:

Edward, as a member of the middle classes, has time to 'while away hours' making plans for the future. Russell shows that the working classes do not have the security to waste precious time on planning for their futures.

> If I was him I'd bring you flowers
> And ask you to dance
> We'd while away the hours making future plans
> For rainy days in country lanes
> And trips to the sea
> I'd just tell you that I love you
> If it was me.

Here we see dance used as a symbol of loving times where couples work in harmony. This use of dance links with the use of 'flowers' as a symbol of romantic love.

Once again we see a character wishing they had the life of another character. In this case, Edward wishes that he could be 'the guy' who openly loves Linda.

With the inclusion of 'rainy days' Russell is using a motif from romantic films and novels where lovers are caught in the rain. Notice how Edward links this romantic image to 'trips to the sea'. In the series of snapshots showing the development of the friendship between Edward, Mickey and Linda over the four year period, there were trips to the sea. Edward obviously remembers these trips fondly.

DO IT!

In this section, we see that Edward loves Linda but he does not say 'a word'. If he had told her that he loved her at this point in the play, what might have been different?

Character and theme essentials

Secrets

Once again we have a host of secrets in this section. Edward challenges his mother when he yells at her following her discovery of the locket: 'It's just a secret, everybody has secrets, don't you have secrets?' It is her secret, of course, that is at the heart of the play. The audience learns from Mrs Johnstone that Mickey does 'secret dancing' in his room and he is uncomfortable that Linda keeps telling everyone that she loves him, as though it should be kept as a secret – like his love for her. Mickey and Edward try to keep it a secret that they are going to see a pornographic film at the cinema. However, Mrs Johnstone guesses and Linda outspokenly tells them that she has been to see the film. Mickey is forced to reveal his secret love for Linda by asking her out, whereas Edward is forced to keep his feelings locked away.

Fairy tales

After Mrs Lyons attacks Mrs Johnstone with the kitchen knife, the local children pick up the narration, chanting tales of the 'mad woman' who lives 'High on the hill'. Mrs Lyons has become the stuff of fairy tales, the woman to avoid: 'Never eat the sweets she gives'. They warn what will happen if 'she catches you eye'. She has become part of local legend.

Edward and Mickey

Edward and Mickey reunite and continue their friendship as they become teenagers. Both are interested in girls, but being at an all-boys school thwarts Edward and Mickey is thwarted by his lack of confidence. Russell shows the audience how both of the boys envy the other's life and looks and, of course, he reveals how they both share a love for the same girl, Linda.

Edward's future is bright with opportunities that a university education will bring. Mickey, at the end of this section of the play, is seen working overtime at a job he hates. These opportunities, or lack of them, Russell attributes to their class background. Edward, a member of the middle classes, has access to opportunities that Mickey does not. However, the family life with a warm but poor mother contrasts sharply with Edward's wealthy but lonely existence with his cold mother and absent father.

Sammy

As Sammy's weapons increase in their lethal nature, so do his crimes. In this section, Russell develops Sammy's criminal actions that will set Mickey on his downward spiral later in the play. In this section Sammy's weapons escalate to a knife, which he pulls on the bus conductor in an argument about paying full fare. That he would behave so threateningly for such a small amount of money enables Russell to suggest how ruthless he has become.

The Narrator/fate

The Narrator continues to stalk Mrs Johnstone and Mrs Lyons in his role as fate, telling them that 'the devil's got your number'. Linda joins the women as she will also 'pay the price' for her part in the developing love triangle.

1   In the opening of Act Two, how does Mrs Johnstone feel about her new house?

2   What dance does Mrs Lyons do with Edward? Why is this important?

3   In this dancing scene, how does Mrs Lyons show that she is scared for their welfare?

4   Who does Mrs Johnstone say that Mickey has been talking about in his sleep? How does he react?

5   The Narrator says that 'no-one gets off without the price being paid' to Mrs Johnstone. What does he mean?

6   How old does Sammy claim to be on the bus?

7   Who stops Mickey from getting off the bus with Sammy? Why is this important?

8   Why does Edward get suspended from school?

9   Why does Mickey get suspended from school?

10   When Mrs Lyons sees the picture in the locket, what is her reaction?

11   Before running from the room to his bedroom, what does Edward yell at his mother?

12   When the Policeman asks the three friends what they 'think you're doin'?', what is their reply?

13   Why is this humorous?

14   The Narrator talks of the things that can be wrong with the beach. What are those things?

15   What do these items on the beach symbolise?

16   Why is Edward leaving Liverpool?

17   What reason does Linda give to Edward for hoping that Mickey never has to ask her to marry him?

18   Edward replies that Mickey is 'mad' to wait so long to ask Linda out, telling her that he would have asked her out years ago. What does she reply?

19   Mickey says that he is going to do overtime so that the Christmas party is on him. What does Edward reply?

20   Why is this deal significant at this point in the play? Explain your ideas.

Act Two:
Fate has its way

A sign of the times

Summary

Mickey tells his mother that Linda is pregnant. She says she is not angry with him and that she'd be a hypocrite if she was. Mr Lyons informs the workforce that due to the recession they are all sacked. All the workers – including Mickey – are now unsuccessfully looking for jobs. (The whole of this scene is presented through actions taking place behind a jolly song. This contrasts light-heartedness and misery, making Mr Lyons' concern for his workforce seem false.)

When Edward, full of enthusiasm, returns from university for Christmas, he finds Mickey depressed and unfriendly. Edward offers Mickey money but this angers Mickey. He calls Edward 'a kid' and threatens to hit him. (Edward again shows his naivety – he doesn't understand why Mickey would consider work 'so important'. Here Edward's naivety might come across as insensitive rather than charming.)

Edward tells Linda he loves her and asks her to marry him. She tells him she is already married and pregnant.

Sammy persuades Mickey to help him carry out an armed robbery in return for 'fifty quid'. Mickey promises Linda that he will take her dancing and dining later that evening. (Fifty pounds is significant: it is the same amount that Mrs Lyons used to pay off Mrs Johnstone after Edward was born. It seals another fatal deal. At the time the play is set in – the 1960s – fifty pounds was a large amount of money – especially to a family as poor as the Johnstones.)

Linda realises where the money will come from and calls to Mickey to stop. He ignores her. Her fear is pointed out by the Narrator. (Compare Linda here with her attitude as a child. Far from daring Mickey to join Sammy in the robbery, she is horrified and tries to stop him.)

What new insights are we given about each character in this section? Complete the table below to explore your ideas. Some ideas have been filled in to get you started.

Character	New insights	Links to themes/ideas/other parts of the play
Linda	She is changing, growing up, becoming more responsible. She is no longer reckless and daring: now she predicts and tries to avoid dangers. She reveals that she has always loved Edward 'in a way'.	As a child – in the park – she was braver and more reckless than the boys, urging them to take risks.

Character	New insights	Links to themes/ideas/other parts of the play
Mrs Johnstone		
Mickey		
Edward		

Language and tone

The 'fading sun' is a metaphor of the beginning of the end of the Johnstones' happiness. Sun is a traditional symbol of joy and hope. 'Fade' shows that the optimism is damaged, not destroyed, yet in unstoppable decline. Winter is approaching and is **personified** as a 'promise-breaker', threatening misery. The neat rhyme 'fade'/'made' gives a tone of inevitability.

> **NARRATOR**: It was one day in October when the sun began to fade,
> And Winter broke the promise that Summer had just made…

A poppet is an affectionate term for a child and is patronising when applied to an adult like Miss Jones. The **alliteration** of the 'p' sounds makes the phrase sound silly and therefore insincere. The childish rhyming of 'poppet' and 'got it' accentuates the insincere tone.

> **MR LYONS** (*singing*): You've been a perfect poppet
> Yes that's right Miss Jones, you've got it
> It's just another sign
> Of the times…

Russell uses Edward's nicknames, his surname and a mock insult to establish the speech patterns of middle-class students' – in contrast to the speech style of the Johnstones. The contrast makes Edward's friends sound trivial and free of responsibility, or like kids (which is what Mickey accused Edward of).

> **EDWARD'S FRIENDS** (*variously; off*): Where's Lyo? Come on Lyons, you pillock… Come on Lyonese…

DO IT!

Read the Narrator's words below. Look carefully at the language used, explain what the Narrator means and consider what an audience might expect to happen.

> There's a black cat stalking and a woman who's afraid,
> That there's no getting off without the price being paid

STRETCH IT!

Imagine you are directing the play. Give some advice to an actor about how you want them to play Mr Lyons *or* the Narrator in this part of the play so as to affect the audience's reaction. Explain your advice.

- Structure your advice around these word stems:

  - At *this point in the play, I want you to imagine that [character's name] is…*

  - *This will make the audience feel that…*

- Continue to give and explain your advice about the actor's performance and how it will help create a particular mood at this point.

- You could give the actor advice about techniques such as gesture and tone.

'The price you're gonna have to pay'

Summary

The raid on the filling station goes wrong: the attendant sets off an alarm and Sammy shoots him. Sammy and Mickey run home and hide the gun. The police arrive and take them away.

(Mickey can't stop crying after Sammy shoots the attendant. Presumably he realises that his foolishness has lost him everything he hoped for.)

Mickey is sentenced to seven years in prison. He slumps into depression and is given pills. As Mickey's release approaches, Linda urges him to give up the pills that have taken away his energy and interest. Mickey tells her he cannot cope without them. (Just as Mr Lyons urged his wife to take pills for her nerves rather than trying to understand and support her, the prison authorities take the same approach with Mickey.)

Mickey is still taking the pills months after returning home. Linda tells Mrs Johnstone that she has found a home for herself and Mickey, and a job for Mickey too. Mrs Johnstone is delighted. Linda refuses to say how she found the home and job, except that she knows someone 'on the housin' committee'. She hopes that now Mickey will give up the pills. (The help that Edward has given to Linda is another example of a 'secret deal' whose debt will have to be repaid at some point. It is another example of living on the 'never never' – buying on credit – that Russell keeps reminding us about through the Narrator: have something now and worry about how it will be paid for later.)

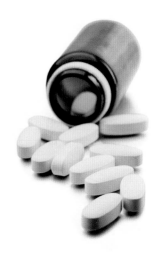

In their new home, as he is about to leave for work, Mickey demands to know where Linda has hidden his pills. He confronts her with the accusation that it was 'Councillor Eddie Lyons' who sorted out the job and their home. He leaves for work with the pills. (Mickey feels humiliated by being dependent on Linda and his old best friend, Edward. Is it his male, working-class pride that has been hurt?)

Linda phones Edward and arranges to meet him in the park. They kiss and hold hands. Meanwhile, at work, Mickey fights the temptation to take his pills. Mrs Lyons tells Mickey that she has seen Edward and Linda together. Mickey goes to his mother's house, gets Sammy's gun and goes out.

Linda and Mickey

Before his release from prison, Linda tries to persuade Mickey to give up his pills.

> **LINDA**: I get depressed but I don't take those. You don't need those, Mickey.
>
> **MICKEY**: Leave me alone, will y'? I can't cope with this. I'm not well. The doctor said, didn't he, I'm not well…I can't do things… leave me alone…

Linda seems to be accusing Mickey of lacking her willpower. Against her accusation, Mickey takes refuge in the advice of an expert – his doctor. He is being defeatist, claiming that he can't pull himself out of his depression. Russell is contrasting Linda's (and Mrs Johnstone's) strength and determination with Mickey's defeatism.

In their new home, Linda angers Mickey by insisting he can give up the pills now they have sorted themselves out.

It's as though Mickey is punishing Linda by taking the pills. Using the official title, 'Councillor', before their old friend Edward's name gives Mickey a tone of hurtful contempt.

Read what one student wrote about Mickey at this point in the play. Notice how the student treats Mickey not as a real person, but as a character created by Russell for particular purposes.

> **MICKEY**: I'm not stupid, Linda. You sorted it out. You an' Councillor Eddie Lyons. *Linda doesn't deny it.* Now give me the tablets…I need them.

> Although you can sympathise with Mickey, there is something pathetic about his self-pity. He seems determined to blame others for his circumstances and make excuses for his weakness. It's as though Russell is making a strong contrast between him and Linda as part of Russell's celebration of the strength of working-class women like Linda and Mrs Johnstone.

NAILIT!

In your AQA exam, make sure you do not write about characters as though they are real people. Characters might be realistic in many ways, but they have been *created* by the writer. Try to mention how particular characters are presented by the writer, and how things they say and do shed light on the focus of the exam question.

AQA exam-style question

How does Russell use the character of Linda to explore ideas about strength and weakness in *Blood Brothers*?

Write about:

- what Linda says and does and what happens to her
- how Russell presents Linda.

[30 marks]

'There's a man gone mad'

Summary

Mickey runs through the town with no clear purpose. Mrs Johnstone can't catch him so she tells Linda what has happened. Linda realises Mickey must be after Edward, and they run to the Town Hall. (As Mickey and his mother run around frantically the Narrator raises the tension by constantly repeating, 'There's a mad man', almost as though he is enjoying the looming disaster.)

Edward is addressing a council meeting when Mickey approaches the platform, pointing the gun at him. The other councillors leave. Mickey accuses Edward of betraying their bond as blood brothers. He even asks Edward if his child is really Edward's. (Mickey is not just upset with Edward for appearing to steal Linda from him. His grievance is deeper: he resents Edward for having everything while he's 'got nothin'. In fact he feels owned by Edward – and presumably by Edward's social class.)

The police arrive and tell Mickey to put the gun down. Mrs Johnstone approaches the platform and tells Mickey that he and Edward are twin brothers, but Mickey becomes enraged with his mother for not having given *him* away instead of Edward. As he waves the gun in Edward's direction it goes off, killing Edward. The police open fire, killing Mickey. (Ironically, in the bloodshed of their violent deaths, Mickey and Edward become literal blood brothers.)

The Narrator asks if class, rather than superstition, caused the deaths. Mrs Johnstone wishes that the shootings were not true but just a story – like in a movie – and that they could just start again. (Mrs Johnstone – joined by the whole **cast** – wishes that the ending was a dream or just a game. It's a fitting end to a play in which the borders between dreams and games, are often mixed up.)

STRETCH IT!

Give at least three explanations for the Narrator's idea that social class might be to blame for the deaths of the twins.

DO IT!

Complete the table below to show how reality and make-believe seem to get mixed up at three points in the play. Some detail has been suggested to get you started.

Point in the play	Exploration
The children's street games in Act One	Each game leads to the next with a mounting violence and explosive power that overwhelms the audience. For example,…

Say it's just a story

> NARRATOR: You know the devil's got your number
> You know he's right beside you
> He's screamin' deep inside you,
> And someone said he's callin' your number up today

Russell has subtly changed the Narrator's familiar lines. The devil is no longer 'behind': he is now 'beside you', meaning he has caught up and is moving in to collect what he's owed. In fact, he's so close that he is 'inside you', and he hasn't just 'got your number' any more: he's dialling it *now*. The effect is chilling and heightens the tension.

Mickey confronts Edward:

> MICKEY: Well, how come you got everything…An' I got nothin' ? (*Pause*) Friends. I've been thinkin' again Eddie. You an' Linda were friends when she first got pregnant, weren't y'?
> EDWARD: Mickey!
> MICKEY: Does my child belong to you as well as everythin' else?

In a sense, as twins, Edward and Mickey must be equals, but Mickey resents having nothing and the feeling that the little he has ever had is only lent by those more fortunate than he is. He doesn't even truly own his own child. Edward's class virtually owns Mickey's life.

The ending

The ending feels satisfying because Russell brings the play in a full circle so that the start of the play now makes full sense. We understand with our intelligence and with our emotions. The twins' deaths fulfil Mrs Lyons' ominous prediction. However, the Narrator asks us to look beyond superstition to see how class inequality might better explain the plot of the play.

Mrs Johnstone is left heartbroken, wishing that the tragic ending was a dream or a game. (And, of course, for us it is! It is a play.) However, what we should also note is that Mrs Johnstone is typically resigned: she wishes life was different, but she is realistic enough to know that tragedy and unhappiness is inevitable – and must be endured.

DO IT!

1 What questions are left unanswered at the end of the play? For example, what happened to Mr and Mrs Lyons? How did they react to the deaths of Edward and Mickey?

2 What do you think Russell wants us to learn by the end of the play? (Consider the themes on the following pages to help you.)
Write a paragraph explaining your ideas.

Character and theme essentials

Class and inequality

The working-class characters are very aware of their hardships and the injustice of the class society they live in. Mickey resents the fact that even basics such as a home and a job are given as favours by Edward (as a representative of the employer class). Edward's father takes away his workers' livings with patronising insincerity. Edward's class takes its advantages for granted and shows no understanding for those who do not share those advantages.

Fate

The tragic ending seems inevitable and the Narrator reminds us that 'the price' will have to be paid. In this last section of the play, the 'devil' has not just got their number, but is calling their number 'today'. All the references to bad luck reinforce this idea of the workings of an evil fate. However, the Johnstones' – and Mickey's and Edward's – fate is determined not by bad luck but by the workings of class inequalities. The border between poverty and affluence is maintained by snobbery and secrecy. Russell shows us that crossing the border from either direction can be fatal.

Women

Linda and Mrs Johnstone are defiant, strong, resourceful, realistic and collaborative. Their 'weaknesses' such as love and occasional recklessness, only make these characters more believable. These two women are the play's heroes.

Mrs Johnstone

Mrs Johnstone shows her wisdom and tolerance when she is not angry with Mickey for getting Linda pregnant. She values their love over 'respectable' behaviour. Even when Linda flirts with Edward she only calls them 'two fools/ Who know the rules' and choose to break them – like she did herself. At the end of the play she is devastated by her twins' deaths, but she sounds sadly resigned to the tragedy: she has the strength to carry on.

Mickey

After the disastrous petrol station robbery, Mickey seems defeated. Unlike his mother, he seems to give up. He sees no point in going on. He is saved by the strength and determination of the women – his wife and his mother. Although he finally tries to fight off his self-pity, jealousy and resentment fuel his final showdown with Edward.

Edward

Mickey accuses Edward of being 'still a kid'. He is right: like a child, Edward is not burdened by responsibilities and hardship. He doesn't understand the value of money because he has plenty of it. This means that he does not fully appreciate the significance of his actions: he meets Linda and kisses her without worrying about what that might lead to. Even when Mickey confronts him with a gun, he can't understand Mickey's feelings. He is an innocent, despite his class advantages.

Linda

Linda is loyal to Mickey throughout his time in prison and she remains focused on solving their problems rather than wallowing in them as Mickey does. When she can no longer take his defeatism, she weakens and seeks relief in a flirtation with Edward. The Narrator and Mrs Johnstone both show understanding for this small expression of freedom.

REVIEW IT!

1 Why is Mrs Johnstone not angry with Mickey for getting Linda pregnant?

2 What reasons does Mr Lyons give for having to close the factory?

3 Who is Miss Jones?

4 What surprises Edward when he returns for Christmas?

5 Why does Mickey accuse Edward of being 'still a kid'?

6 How does Sammy persuade Mickey to help him with the petrol station robbery?

7 How does the robbery go wrong?

8 How does Mickey cope with his misery in prison?

9 Why is Mickey released from prison before the end of his sentence?

10 How does Linda get a new home and a job for Mickey?

11 Why does Linda arrange to meet Edward?

12 What do Edward and Linda do at their meeting?

13 What does Mickey take from his mother's house?

14 What is Edward doing when Mickey finds him?

15 How does Mrs Johnstone try to persuade Mickey not to shoot Edward?

16 How does Mickey react to the information Mrs Johnstone gives him?

17 What effect on the audience does Russell create through the 'sacking song' that is begun by Mr Lyons and taken up by the whole cast?

18 How do you think we should feel about how Mickey reacts to his imprisonment?

19 Do you think Willy Russell wants us to believe in Mrs Lyons' superstition about what would happen if twins discovered their other halves?

20 Does the play end well? Could it have ended better? Explain.

Characters

Mrs Johnstone

What we know about Mrs Johnstone

- Mrs Johnstone opens and closes the play, singing 'Tell me it's not true'.

- She is 25 at the start of the play but looks older. She once looked like 'Marilyn Monroe'.

- She has lots of children and her husband has left her, leaving her in poverty. Despite this material poverty, she is rich in children.

- In desperation, she gives one of her twin boys to Mrs Lyons to raise as her own son.

- She is superstitious and believes Mrs Lyons' made-up superstition without question.

- She loves her children, feeling guilt and regret for giving Edward to Mrs Lyons.

- She tries to remain cheerful even in the face of difficult times.

Write a paragraph explaining your own view of Mrs Johnstone at the end of the play.

Mrs Johnstone as a mother

At the start of the play, Mrs Johnstone is presented as facing grinding poverty, yet remaining hopeful that she will regain the happiness symbolised by going dancing. Russell presents her as showing no bitterness towards the husband who has abandoned her and their many children for a younger version of herself 'who looks a bit like Marilyn Monroe'.

Mrs Lyons

What do we know about Mrs Lyons?

- Mrs Lyons, unable to have children, wants a baby.

- She manipulates Mrs Johnstone into parting with one of her twin babies by telling her that the 'Welfare people' will take her children as she doesn't have the means to look after them. She preys on Mrs Johnstone's superstitious nature and then gets to her to swear an oath on the Bible.

- She is wealthy and doesn't need to work, yet her husband is distant towards her.

- She is guilty about the deceit involved in taking Edward, but this turns into suspicion, fear and paranoia.

- She is not superstitious but the events she sets in motion are ruled by fate.

- Her fear leads to her reacting violently – once towards Edward, when she hits him, and once towards Mrs Johnstone with a knife.

- She betrays Edward and Linda by telling Mickey about them with fatal results.

Does Russell want us to see Mrs Lyons as naturally cold and unhappy, or as a person who *becomes* cold and unhappy through circumstances and the choices she has made in her life? Her marriage appears to be hollow with her absent husband, even though she has an array of wealth with a large house and access to money. However, even when she achieves her greatest desire – a baby – she does not enjoy the luxury of that child. Instead she feels unsafe knowing that one day she will have to 'pay the price' for what she has done. The 'devil has her number'.

How do *we* feel about Mrs Lyons?

Surely Mrs Lyons' betrayal of her own son at the end of Act Two when she goes to the factory to see Mickey appals everyone, yet she does have some strengths: she is clever enough to know exactly how to manipulate Mrs Johnstone and is delighted when she thinks that the locket is from 'a girlfriend'. Of course, how we feel about Mrs Lyons depends on who 'we' are. She is loathsome, scheming and manipulative. However she is also a character we feel sorry for: she is neglected by her husband; she is bored by her life and the one thing she desperately wants, she can't have. The play was viewed by critics as being profoundly moving when it was first shown in theatres.

NAILIT!

In your AQA exam, it is worth considering how attitudes towards Mrs Lyons might differ, so do not jump to conclusions. Keep an open mind.

DOIT!

Look at this list of words that *might* be appropriate to Mrs Lyons:

manipulative   desperate   protective   unbalanced   violent   brave   determined   deserted   evil

1 Think carefully about these nine words and put them into a rank order from the most to the least true. You might find that the top half of your rank order contains both negative and positive words.

2 Find evidence to support your top three word choices.

Mickey Johnstone

What we know about Mickey

- Mickey is the twin who grows up in the working-class Johnstone family.

- We first meet him when he is seven, wishing he were older and unhappy that his older brother gets to do things that he isn't allowed to do.

- At the start of the play he is open and friendly towards Edward. He suggests that they become 'blood brothers' and he is keen to introduce his new friend to his mother and later Linda.

- As the play continues, we see Mickey begin to change. As a teenager he is awkward about how he feels for Linda but once he does kiss her in Act Two, Russell presents Linda remarking, 'Y' take y' time getting going but then there's no stoppin' y'.' This is the high point of Mickey's life. From this point onwards his life begins its descent towards its fatal end.

- Linda's pregnancy and losing his job marks a turning point for Mickey. It is from this point that he is caught up in Sammy's criminal activity that leads to his imprisonment and dependency on antidepressants.

NAILIT!

To do well in your AQA exam, you need to develop and defend your own view of the characters:

- to what extent are they *victims* of outside influences, poverty, class and of their own weaknesses?

- can we feel any sympathy for them?

How should we feel about Mickey?

It could be argued that Mickey's tragedy is caused by allowing himself to be manipulated by Mrs Lyons – just like his mother allowed Mrs Lyons to prey on her. However, it could also be argued that Mickey is a victim of his times. In the 1980s, when the play was first performed, Britain faced the decline of the manufacturing industry. This is the industry Mickey depends on for a living. His struggles were faced by many millions of people in the country, but especially those in the north, including Liverpool. Willy Russell wanted to point out that Margaret Thatcher's ideal that everyone who works hard can do well was a lie. (Margaret Thatcher was prime minister in the 1980s). Mickey is presented as hard-working but does not have the same opportunities as Edward who is unaffected by events.

Here are some words, which *might* be used about Mickey in the play:

> open   optimistic   unhappy   self-doubting   cynical
> desperate   mischievous   honest   broken

- Choose the two words from the list above that you think are *most* true of Mickey

- Explain your choices with reference the play.

- Does your choice differ at different points in the play?

STRETCHIT!

What other words could be used to sum up Mickey? Choose two words not on the list above and explain why they are particularly true of Mickey.

Edward Lyons

What do we know about Edward?

- Edward is the twin who grows up in the middle-class family.

- At the start of the play, Edward is shown as open, generous and in awe of Mickey and Linda.

- He shows his loyalty to Mickey through his blood bond and wearing the locket that Mrs Johnstone gives him. He continues to wear this despite the trouble it causes him both at school and through his mother. He is also loyal to Mickey by not saying 'a word' of his feelings for Linda until later in the play.

- Edward has the advantages of an expensive education and entrance to a prestigious university, but his family life is not ideal. His father is absent and distant and his mother is cold.

- Through Linda's request, he tries to help Mickey with a job and a house but also embarks on an affair with Linda. This leads to Mickey's actions at the end of the play causing his death.

Writing about Russell's presentation of Edward

Read part of what one student wrote about Edward. Notice how the student uses evidence to support their points:

> I don't know how I feel about Edward. I know that he tried to help Mickey when Mickey needed a job and a house, but I also know that he can do this from a position of privilege as 'Councillor Lyons' who 'sorted it out'. This position was open to him because of his education and probably the self-belief his middle-class upbringing gave him. In Act Two, when the friends are eighteen, we know that he will not show his love for Linda, even prompting Mickey to ask her out. However, this selfless attitude does not continue, for later in the act he embarks on 'a light romance' with Linda. Russell presents Mickey as being in a terrible place mentally and presents Edward betraying his 'blood-brother' in the worst possible way.

NAILIT!

In your AQA exam, when you write about a character, make sure you make clear points in answer to the question and back up your points by referring to events and language in the play.

DO IT!

- Look at the mark scheme on page 86. Give special attention to the criteria for choosing and using evidence.

- What are the strengths of the answer above?

- Give the student some brief advice about how to improve their answer.

Linda

What do we know about Linda?

- Linda is a friend of Mickey's and together they draw Edward into their group. At the start, we see Linda as strong as she deflects bullets with a bin lid in the children's games, yet she is compassionate as she allays Mickey's fears of death.

- Linda stands up to Sammy even as a child and sees him for the threat he represents: 'He's always been a soft get, your Sammy.'

- Linda is frank about her love for Mickey during their teenage years despite Mickey's shyness and reserve.

- Linda remains loyal during Mickey's prison sentence and tries to get him to stop taking the antidepressants: 'When you take those things, Mickey, I can't even see you.'

- Linda becomes the love interest in the love triangle between Edward and Mickey.

- When Mickey loses his job and is in the depths of depression, Linda turns to Edward for help. They begin a 'light romance'.

NAILIT!

When writing about characters, remember that Russell created them for a purpose. They are a construct – they are not real people.

DOIT!

What do you think are the five most important things to remember about Linda?

- Find three quotations.

- Link Linda to Russell's social message.

How should we feel about Linda?

Like Mrs Johnstone, Linda can be viewed as one of the heroes of the play. The strong and independent women in his family that he was surrounded by influenced Willy Russell. Many of his lead working-class female characters, such as Rita in *Educating Rita* or Shirley in *Shirley Valentine,* are presented as showing dignity, strength and resilience in the face of their circumstances. Linda is one of these characters. Linda's affair with Edward represents the betrayal that happens when hope is lost and only desperation and bleak times remain.

Sammy Johnstone

What do we know about Sammy?

- Sammy Johnstone is Mickey's older brother by two years.

- As a ten-year-old, Sammy's behaviour is outlined as: 'robbin'' toy cars, spitting and 'playing with matches'. Mickey sets his behaviour as 'dead mean' right from the start.

- Sammy's love of weapons is shown as increasing in threat from a toy gun, to an air pistol, to a knife, to a shotgun.

- During the play, Sammy burns down the school, pulls a knife on a bus conductor when he doesn't want to pay full fare and kills during a robbery.

- Linda stands up to him as a child, threatening to tell her mother 'why all her ciggies disappear' when Sammy is around, causing him to back down and leave. At the end of the play, she tries to stop Mickey from joining Sammy for the robbery, but fatally, this time, she fails to protect him.

How should we feel about Sammy?

Sammy's influence on other children is to cause them to suspect any generous action. This corrosive effect is seen in the episode with the sweets. Here Mickey is suspicious of Edward's generosity with the sweets, as he has learned that appearances are deceptive from Sammy who would have 'weed' on them presumably so that he could cynically watch the innocent recipients taking one of them.

Sammy has had the same upbringing as Mickey and has the same genes as both Mickey and Edward. Despite this, he is completely different to both of them. In terms of the nature versus nurture debate, he shows that it is neither your genetic make-up (nature) nor the way you are brought up (nurture) that makes you behave in a corrupt or antisocial way. Russell suggests that Sammy's nature is due to the plate in his head – received when he fell out of a window when Donna Marie was 'looking after' him, while his mother was at work. So, Russell's point is that his antisocial behaviour stems from his accident rather than the influence of his class.

NAILIT!

In your AQA exam, think about how different ways characters have been used by Russell to present his social message. Use tentative words such as 'perhaps', 'might', 'could be' to help you consider more than one view of a character or theme.

DOIT!

In a parallel scene where Sammy persuades Mickey to act as lookout for the robbery, we also see Edward meeting up with Linda. What do these scenes have in common?

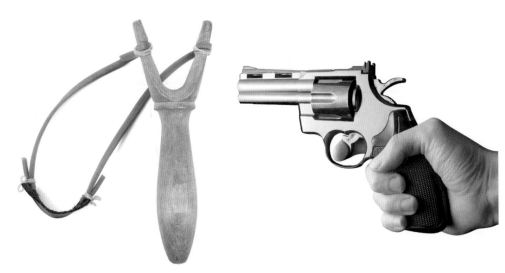

The Narrator

The Narrator appears as omniscient (all seeing and all knowing). He is on stage at all times and fulfils the same function as the chorus in ancient Greek tragedies (see also page 82).

The Narrator is key to the action of the play and carries out the functions below.

The Narrator **takes on various roles** according to the needs of the plot. For example, he appears as a milkman, a bus conductor and teachers.

The Narrator **reminds the audience of the initial deal** that was made by Mrs Johnstone and Mrs Lyons and as the voice of fate, issuing warnings of what is to come.

> Now there's no going back, for anyone.
> It's too late now, for feeling torn
> There's a pact been sealed, there's a deal been born.

The Narrator **watches the action** alongside the audience and points out interesting or noteworthy incidents:

> So did y' hear the story of the Johnstone twins?
> As like each other as two new pins,
> Of one womb born, on the self same day,
> How one was kept and one given away?

The Narrator

The Narrator **poses the final question to the audience:**

> And do we blame superstition for what came to pass?
> Or could it be what we, the English, have come to know as class?

The Narrator **points out important issues to the characters:**

> You're always gonna know what was done
> Even when you shut your eyes you still see
> That you sold a son
> And you can't tell anyone.

DO IT!

Research the term **'fourth wall'**. How could you apply this to the Narrator in *Blood Brothers*? What is the effect of this type of narration?

REVIEW IT!

1. Who is known as the most superstitious character?

2. How does Mrs Lyons persuade Mrs Johnstone to give her one of the twins?

3. 'He's dead mean sometimes.' Who is being described here?

4. How does Sammy react to Edward when he first meets him?

5. During the children's games in Act One, Linda appears as a 'Moll' in one of the scenes. What is that and why is it significant?

6. When Mickey confesses to being afraid of death, Linda gives him two reasons not to worry about it. What are they?

7. When Linda and Mickey set off to the park with Sammy's air pistol, what are they planning to do?

8. What does this plan tell the audience about Linda?

9. Mr Lyons suggests that Mrs Lyons should get 'something for your nerves' when she tells him that she is worried about Edward. What does this show about his character?

10. Who has 'no reputation following me'? Explain the circumstances.

11. Look at this quotation about Edward by his teacher:

> " Getting rather big for your boots, aren't you? "

Why does the teacher say this? Is he right? Explain your ideas.

12. In three words, describe Mickey.

13. In three words, describe Edward.

14. In three words, describe Linda.

15. How does Linda describe the boy looking out of the window? Why is this significant?

16. Linda leaves angrily. How does Mickey react?

17. What colour is Edward's hair? What is Mickey's?

18. Mr Lyons is shown sending letters to his workforce as he ends their contracts. What does he represent here?

19. When Edward tries to help Mickey when he realises that Mickey is out of work, how does Mickey react?

20. Look at Mickey's last speech to Edward before Linda enters. What effect was Russell trying to achieve?

Themes and contexts

What do we mean by 'theme'?

In literature a theme is a central idea that the writer illustrates and explores through their text. A theme does not have to be as strong as a 'message' – something definite that the writer is trying to teach the reader. A theme can just be a topic or concern that a writer clearly has in mind as they write and develop their text. This section sums up some of the key themes that run throughout *Blood Brothers*.

Secrets

Secret deals threaten disaster throughout the play. The first secret 'pact' or 'deal' is the one between Mrs Lyons and Mrs Johnstone. Russell makes the audience apprehensive about this agreement by accompanying it with '*a bass note*' like '*a heartbeat*' that repeats in a crescendo while the Narrator warns us that 'there's no going back', implying that a chain of events has been set off that the two women will not be able to control. Although this secret 'selling' of a baby is the springboard for all the play's action, other secret deals refuel the plot's journey to disaster. These include Mickey's agreement to help Sammy in the petrol station robbery, and the help that Edward gives Linda in finding a home and a job for Mickey.

Bonds, trust and betrayal

There are some important examples of personal bonds in the play: a mother's with her children; a wife and husband, and, of course, the natural bond between twin brothers. Mickey and Edward are unaware of this bond but they sense it, and they formalise it in their blood brothers' ceremony. Mickey insists that this bonding means they 'always have to stand by each other' and defend each other. Mickey goes against this agreement by rejecting Edward when he returns from university. Later, Edward seems to betray the bond completely by his secret liaison with Mickey's wife.

Name at least two other secrets in the play and briefly explain how they contribute to the tragic ending.

Writing about trust and betrayal in *Blood Brothers*

See how one student tries to establish a clear and original point about the significance of trust and betrayal in *Blood Brothers.* An examiner has made some notes alongside.

> You could say that Edward's feelings for Linda don't undermine his bond with Mickey, but confirm it. Half-jokingly, Mickey finishes the bonding ceremony by telling Edward that part of the agreement is that blood brothers must share their sweets. This is a childish focus for sharing, but as the twins grow up, they share Linda as a friend. The Narrator photographs them grouped together, arms round each other'. At their happiest they are united, happy to share each other. In a way Edward shares Linda with Mickey by making him ask her out. They both thank Edward for this. So, perhaps Russell doesn't want us to see Edward's secret meeting with Linda as a betrayal at all.

Clear and plausible point of view.

Evidence and examples support the point of view.

Explanations of the significance of the evidence is offered.

Restatement of the point in the light of the argument and evidence offered. Giving consideration to Russell's intention moves beyond mere personal response.

Debt

When Mrs Johnstone and Mrs Lyons make their pact of secrecy, the Narrator warns us that 'a debt is a debt and must be paid'. In other words, all agreements need to be kept in the end, and they all involve a payment of some sort. It is often said that debts 'hang over' people who owe money: it is as though they are a constant, oppressive threat. The audience is always conscious of the weight of the mysterious debt that hovers over the Johnstones and the Lyons. Of course, Mrs Johnstone's debts are very real: her catalogue debts are often paid by the confiscation of all her possessions.

DO IT!

In Act Two when the boys are finding money for the cinema, the Narrator sings – presumably about Mrs Lyons:

> Did you forget you've got some debts to pay,
> Did you forget about the reckoning day.

Explain how these lines make the idea of debt sound sinister and threatening.

STRETCH IT!

Find two or three of the play's references to debts and 'reckonings'. Write a paragraph explaining how Russell uses these references to build tension in the play.

Social class

At the end of the play, the Narrator asks the audience if class is to blame for the tragic events. He implies that the answer is yes.

What does Willy Russell mean by class?

The Johnstones are a working-class family. They are too poor to own their own home and they are trapped in poverty. They rely on very insecure jobs to make a living and they have very little control over the forces that affect their lives. The Lyons are a well-off middle-class family. They own their own home and have a great deal of control over their own lives, their futures and over the lives of working-class people who work for them – as cleaners or as factory workers. Edward and Mickey are twins, yet very unequal. Through this device of twins separated at birth, Russell is able to show that being wealthy and powerful (rather than poor and powerless) is a matter of luck, not natural superiority, which links to his beliefs in social equality.

Nature versus nurture debate

There have been many studies of twins separated at birth. The point of interest is whether twins achieve equally even though they have been raised in different circumstances. Russell – through the contrasting fortunes of Edward and Mickey – suggests that it is their class background (nurture) that determines an individual's prospects, not their 'natural' talents (nature).

The circumstances of each twin's upbringing (nurture) are significant at every point of their young lives. Edward is drawn towards a high-status education that gives him even more power and influence, while Mickey is drawn towards a life of crime and imprisonment. On the other hand, the respectability and expectations of Edward's upbringing are suffocating and make him long for the freedom to swear, to defy authority and to have adventures for which he envies Mickey.

DO IT!

Find at least two examples of how the Johnstones and the Lyons show their different social classes through the way they speak. Briefly describe the differences between the two styles of speech.

STRETCH IT!

Explain how the differences between the Johnstones' and the Lyons' use of language affects how the audience (or reader) feels about the characters.

AQA exam-style question

'Could it be what we, the English, have come to know as class?'

What does Russell have to say about the effects of social class in *Blood Brothers*?

Write about:

- what characters do and say
- how Russell uses the characters' words and actions to explore ideas about the effects of social class.

[30 marks]

Fate

Being 'fated' means being unable to escape what is going to happen to you. It means having no real control over your life. It is as though fate is hunting Mrs Johnstone down:

> **NARRATOR**: ...y' know the devil's got your number He's gonna find y'...

The 'devil' is the **personification** of the fate triggered by Mrs Johnstone's unwise deals with Mrs Lyons, and with the catalogue companies. The Narrator makes this personification even more sinister by informing us that 'he's knocking at your door'.

Of course, in *Blood Brothers* Mrs Lyons is just as trapped by fate as Mrs Johnstone is, and before long the Narrator applies the same terrifying devil-fate personification to Mrs Lyons, using exactly the same words. The fate Mrs Lyons dreads is driven by her insecurity and her guilt: it is that Edward will be lured away from her, or he will die according to the superstition that when separated twins discover that they are brothers, they die immediately.

Think about yourself and your own family. How much control over your lives and futures do you and your family have? Have you or family members ever done (or not done) something in the past that has had a big impact on the future?

Thinking about these questions will help you to appreciate Willy Russell's views on the significance of fate and restriction in characters' lives.

After the twins' violent deaths, the Narrator asks if 'we blame superstition for what came to pass?' The implication is that we don't: what appears to be fate is a convenient explanation for the nasty workings of the English class system that poisons lives and hopes and turns people against one another.

AQA exam-style question

How does Russell use the character of the Narrator to present the idea of fate?

Write about:

- the role of fate in the play and what the Narrator suggests about it
- how Russell presents fate through what the Narrator says and does.

[30 marks]

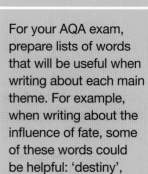

NAILIT!

For your AQA exam, prepare lists of words that will be useful when writing about each main theme. For example, when writing about the influence of fate, some of these words could be helpful: 'destiny', 'forced', 'doom', 'fortune', 'inevitable'.

DOIT!

Plan five paragraph subtopics to fit into the focus of the AQA exam-style question. For example, one could be:

- how the Narrator's choice of words makes fate sound inevitable and sinister.

DOIT!

Poverty

Through the Johnstones, Willy Russell shows the reality and the effects of poverty. The reality is that the family often has to go hungry. The *effects* (results) of that poverty include crime, debt and depression.

What other effects of poverty are suggested by Willy Russell? You could start by considering what one of the Johnstone children says:

> 'Ey Mam, how come I'm on free dinners? All the other kids laugh at me.

Mrs Johnstone's husband escapes poverty by abandoning his own family and going back to acting like a single man with no responsibilities. For his wife and children there is no escape.

As a temporary solution to poverty, Mrs Johnstone gets food and goods on credit. She has no choice. The people she owes money to are not very sympathetic. For example, when she pleads with the Milkman not to stop deliveries, he firmly rejects her plea: 'no money, no milk'. The people owed money seem heartless, but we know that they cannot afford to let Mrs Johnstone have their goods for free: they too have to live.

Russell does not blame individuals for poverty: instead he blames inequality and the social 'system'. By threatening to take away her children rather than helping Mrs Johnstone to feed them, 'the Welfare' is being cruel. When Mrs Lyons forces Mrs Johnstone to give up one of her babies, she seems to be offering a logical solution to Mrs Johnstone's immediate problem. Of course, in reality Mrs Lyons is exploiting Mrs Johnstone's poverty to get what she wants. She could help Mrs Johnstone better by giving her money.

Russell shows how poverty becomes a problem for those who are not suffering it: the Johnstone children are lawless, and when they are rehoused, their neighbours look forward to less crime, noise and graffiti. Russell is not sentimental about poor people: Mickey's brother, Sammy, for example, is a thoroughly unpleasant person.

However, the idea that the poor are to blame for their own poverty is challenged head on through the character of Mrs Johnstone: she works very hard, and however dire her circumstances, she remains constructive and never uses poverty as an excuse for poor behaviour by her children.

AQA exam-style question

What ideas about poverty does Russell explore in the play *Blood Brothers*?

Write about:

- how Russell uses different characters and their reactions to poverty
- how Russell presents these ideas by the ways he writes.

[30 marks]

Women

Linda and Mrs Johnstone are created very sympathetically: it's easy for the audience to admire their qualities *and* understand and forgive any weaknesses they might have. However, Mrs Lyons – despite her problems and unhappiness – is a much less sympathetic character. She is jealous and willing to use force of various kinds to get what she wants.

AQA exam-style question

How far do you agree that Russell presents women as heroes in *Blood Brothers*?

Write about:

- what sorts of women Russell presents in the play
- how Russell presents these women by the ways he writes.

[30 marks]

'I cannot abide being in all-male company. I want to talk about things that matter.' Willy Russell *The Telegraph,* 15 October 2012.

Briefly explain how Willy Russell's view of women and men comes across in *Blood Brothers*.

Read the paragraph below from one student's answer. An examiner has made some notes alongside.

However, in some respects, even Mrs Johnstone cannot be seen as a hero. Firstly, she seems very naive. For example, she 'found' she was pregnant again - as though this had no connection to her behaviour. Then she calls Edward and Linda's secret liaison a mere meeting between 'two fools'. She fails to foresee the fatal consequences of this 'light romance'. Secondly, Mrs Johnstone seems to be too accepting of her circumstances. She even sacrifices her own comfort to help those who are already comfortable. She assures Mrs Lyons that she won't inconvenience her by taking a single day off for maternity, and she predicts that if she ever meets her lost son again, she'll keep silent: 'What's gone before/will be concealed.' 'Will be' emphasises a deliberate act of self-sacrifice on her part: she will put the interests of Edward and his 'mother' above her own. Of course, if these are examples of Mrs Johnstone's weaknesses, they also make her a more believable, imperfect character. Perhaps this ordinariness makes her heroism all the more powerful.

Notice how this student starts by making a clear point that is directly relevant to the exam question.

The student then backs up their point with textual references. Some of those direct references (quotations) are neatly built into the student's own sentences.

Useful exploration of the **connotations** of words.

The paragraph ends with an original insight into what might have been Russell's subtle intentions.

The play's meaning

What do we mean by 'meaning'?

No play has one fixed 'message'. When we talk about the meaning of *Blood Brothers,* we need to *interpret* the play. To do that, we need to think about a few things.

What might be important to Willy Russell

Willy Russell was brought up in working-class Liverpool. Experiencing the injustice of the class system made Russell frustrated and angry. These ideas and feelings are personified in *Blood Brothers* in the struggles of the Johnstone family and in the different fortunes of the two twins. The plot of the play is designed to highlight injustice and inequality.

How the play affects the audience

How the play affects the audience is partly influenced by who the audience is. It is probably significant that in its original form, the first performance of the play was not to an educated, well-off, adult audience, but to secondary school students in Liverpool.

NAIL IT!

When writing about *Blood Brothers* for your AQA exam, don't be afraid to consider more than one interpretation of the play – or a part of it. Keeping an open mind will help you to look carefully at details in the text that support the question focus, rather than simply trotting out ready-made opinions. To help keep an open mind, practise using tentative words and phrases such as 'this might/could suggest', 'perhaps...', 'on the other hand...'

DO IT!

Here are some possible meanings of *Blood Brothers*:
- It is upbringing, not birth, that most influences your chances in life.
- Girls and young women should use contraception if they do not plan to become pregnant and not blame others if they do get pregnant.
- Snobbery and inequality are evils in our society.
- We are all responsible for one another.
- Poor people have only got themselves to blame for their poverty.
- Fate controls our lives.
- It is important to hang on to your dreams of a better life.
- Children should not be treated as possessions.
- Underneath our class differences, we are all the same.

Think about each of these possible meanings. Put them into rank order from most important meaning to the least. Leave out any meanings that you think are not suggested by *Blood Brothers*.

STRETCH IT!

Add your own meanings to the rank order.

- Write brief explanations of your top two choices. Refer to details in the play to support your explanations.
- Do you think that different sorts of audience members might come up with different rank orders?

Context

Some background to the ideas in *Blood Brothers*

The action of *Blood Brothers* begins in the late 1960s in Liverpool, where Willy Russell grew up, the son of a former miner. The play was first performed at the beginning of the 1980s, although Willy Russell had been working on it since the late 1970s.

In 1979 Margaret Thatcher became prime minister. She set out to confront the trade unions and to reduce their power. The unions had grown up over the previous century to defend and extend the rights and living standards of the working class.

The social and political conflict in the early 1980s is an important **context** for the ideas Russell explores in *Blood Brothers*. The play asks questions that are still important but seemed particularly urgent at the time: who or what is to blame for poverty and inequality? Do poor people deserve their poverty? Have rich people earned their advantages? Margaret Thatcher later angered many people with her statement that 'there is no such thing as society', only individuals who should help themselves – and each other. Many – perhaps unfairly – saw these words as a celebration of greed and heartlessness. Certainly many rich and powerful people were encouraged by Thatcher's words to blame poverty on poor people's unwillingness to change their ways and to help themselves. Willy Russell explains that his own father's life 'would have been fantastically different if he'd been born into my generation or into a different class' and that 'is what *Blood Brothers* is about.' (*Blood Brothers*, Willy Russell, Bloomsbury, UK, 2017 pages x–xi)

Some background to the drama of *Blood Brothers*

Blood Brothers feels like a very modern play. However, it is influenced by some much older forms of drama. The lack of scenery, the very dramatic events and the use of a narrator to comment on them so as to guide the audience's reactions has clearly been influenced by the theatre of ancient Greece, which is more than two thousand years old. Ancient Greek theatre often presented the workings of fate and the tragedies that arise when characters fail or refuse to accept their destinies.

Other dramatic influences probably include Shakespeare's *Romeo and Juliet* that presents the tragic consequences of secret bonds and which – like *Blood Brothers* – begins with a summary of what will happen in the play. More recently, J.B. Priestley's famous play, *An Inspector Calls,* also teaches its audiences the importance of social responsibility: 'we are responsible for each other'.

Writing about contexts

In your AQA exam, context means one or all of the following:

- ideas and influences at the time the play was written
- ideas and expectations a modern audience or reader might bring to the play
- how a small detail in the play fits into the whole play.

Here are parts of two different students' answers to a question about what Russell has to say about the effects of social class. The references to context are underlined:

Student answer A

Through the plot of *Blood Brothers*, Russell clearly suggests that the advantages or disadvantages you have in your life are due to the accident of your class background. <u>In terms of the nature versus nurture debate, Russell comes down on the side of nurture (upbringing), not nature (your genetic inheritance).</u>

Student answer B

Willy Russell would have known about the nature versus nurture debate. He was brought up in working-class Liverpool.

Answer B will probably make you think, 'and your point is?' The contextual information given might be correct, but it is not helpful. In fact, it is all context and no comment. By contrast, the contextual information in answer A *adds* to our understanding of the play by shedding light on the significance of a key idea in the play.

You will have noticed that in this *GCSE 9-1 AQA English Literature Study Guide*, contextual information is only referred to when it might enrich your understanding of the play. A typical AQA exam-style question where context could be used might be:

AQA exam-style question

How does Willy Russell present the power of hopes and desires in *Blood Brothers*?

'The power of hopes and desires' is a clear focus of the question. How Russell presents this is partly a matter of *your thoughtful interpretation*. You *might* partly assess Russell's attitude to the power of hopes and desires in the context of:

- the restrictions on people's lives imposed by the class system, and/or
- what *you* think about how much freedom individuals have to fulfil their potential.

REVIEW IT!

1 Which one of the following is the best definition of 'theme'?

   a Something the play is about.

   b Music at the start of the play.

   c The order in which things happen in the play.

2 Give three other words that mean (or roughly mean) 'fate'.

3 Give three other words that mean (or roughly mean) 'secret'.

4 Give three other words that mean (or roughly mean) 'poverty'.

5 Give three other words that mean (or roughly mean) 'inequality'.

6 Name three characters who are socially and economically advantaged.

7 Why does Mrs Johnstone fear that 'the Welfare' might take her children away?

8 What does Mrs Johnstone distrust about 'easy terms'?

9 What does the Narrator mean by 'the devil's got your number'?

10 How does Mrs Johnstone feel about her husband for abandoning his family?

11 Here are five themes: women, fate, class, poverty, secrets.
Which two of these themes are most relevant to the following quotation?

> **MICKEY**: I'd crawl back to that job for half the pay.

(Act Two after Mickey has been unemployed for months.)

12 Give three examples in the play of a character showing concern about another character's desperate situation.

13 Explain the significance of the Policeman describing Edward's behaviour in the park as 'more of a prank really'.

14 Give another example of prejudice in the play.

15 The Narrator warns that the devil's 'staring through your windows,/He's creeping down the hall.' How are these words particularly effective at conveying a sense of the workings of fate?

16 Choose one part of the play (of no more than nine lines) that is very relevant to the theme of class and inequality. Write a paragraph to explain the relevance of those lines.

17 Choose one part of the play (of no more than nine lines) that is very relevant to the theme of hopes and dreams. Write a paragraph to explain the relevance of those lines.

18 Choose one part of the play (of no more than nine lines) that is very relevant to the theme of women. Write a paragraph to explain the relevance of those lines.

19 Choose one part of the play (of no more than nine lines) that is very relevant to the theme of secrets. Write a paragraph to explain the relevance of those lines.

20 Choose one part of the play (of no more than nine lines) that is very relevant to a theme of your choice. Write a paragraph to explain the relevance of those lines.

Language, structure and form

Find recordings of the Liverpool accent and dialect. How successful is Willy Russell in recreating the accent on the page?

Language

The language of class

Understanding the contrast between the lives of working-class people and the lives of middle-class people is key to your understanding of *Blood Brothers*. Russell shows the class of the characters through his realistic use of language, both through structures and vocabulary choices.

Russell quickly establishes the working-class lives of the Johnstone family through a section of dialogue that is heard offstage, showing the audience what it would have been like to live as neighbours to this family. The poverty and the class of this family is also established through this dialogue. The audience is left in no doubt that these children are hungry because the cupboards are empty.

Russell uses abbreviated words to show the Liverpool accent – often the dropped 'g' or 'd' at the end of words.

Notice how many ways Russell names Mrs Johnstone here, immediately establishing that she is the mother of many children. It is interesting that the more middle-class 'Mummy' is not used.

The language choices are informal with colloquial terms used.

> **KID ONE** (*off*): Mam, Mam, the baby's cryin'. He wants his bottle. Where's the milk?
> **KID TWO** (*off*): 'Ey Mam, how come I'm on free dinners? All the other kids laugh at me.
> **KID THREE** (*off*): 'Ey Mother, I'm starvin' an' there's nothin' in. There never bloody well is.
> **MRS JOHNSTONE** (*perfunctorily*): Don't swear, I've told y'.
> **KID FOUR** (*off*): Mum, I can't sleep, I'm hungry, I'm starvin'...
> **KIDS** (*off*): An' me, Mam. An' me. An' me

Here we see the casual use of swearing by the Johnstone family. This sets them apart from the Lyons family, but delights Edward when he meets them, as it is exciting and new. Notice that Mrs Johnstone responds '*perfunctorily*'. This means that she says the words because she thinks she needs to, but she doesn't really mean it. Therefore the children will continue to swear.

Look at the first two lines from Mrs Lyons in the play. How does Willy Russell show that she is of a different class to Mrs Johnstone through the language choices and the content of what she says?

> MRS LYONS: Hello, Mrs Johnstone, how are you? Is the job working out all right for you?
> ...
> MRS LYONS: It's a pretty house isn't it? It's a pity it's so big. I'm finding it rather large at present.

Willy Russell's use of language to increase dramatic tension

The play is built on the audience's knowledge that this is a march towards death for the two boys, for we have seen this in the opening *'re-enactment of the final moments of the play'*. This use of dramatic **irony** increases tension as the audience knows that whatever happiness the characters experience, it will be a fleeting pleasure, like the pleasure found in dancing. Using this knowledge, and supported by his language choices, Russell develops tensions between characters to show how this march begins.

Look at this extract between Mrs Lyons and Edward. Notice how Russell uses language to increase dramatic tension.

DO IT!

Find a scene where Russell uses language to increase dramatic tension. Write a paragraph to show your ideas.

Edward is equally direct in response to his mother's control. He does stand up to her, but does it through the cloak of secrecy. The use of 'secret' links this episode to the central secret within the play: the secret that will always come to the surface.

This is a direct question revealing the sharpness of Mrs Lyons' tone. Her controlling nature, always close to the surface, is evident immediately.

Mrs Lyons' relief is clear as she weaves a narrative in her mind –

'I know' – to explain Edward's discomfort. Russell's use of dramatic irony has the audience waiting for the revelation to Mrs Lyons of the content of the locket.

MRS LYONS: Where did you get this?
EDWARD: I can't tell you that. It's a secret.
MRS LYONS (*finally smiling in relief*): I know it's from a girlfriend, isn't it? (*She laughs.*) Is there a picture in here?
EDWARD: Yes, Mummy. Can I have it back now?
MRS LYONS: You won't let Mummy see your girl friend. Oh, Edward, don't be so… (*She playfully moves away.*) Is she beautiful?
EDWARD: Mummy can…
MRS LYONS: Oh, let me look, let me look. (*She beams a smile at him and then opens the locket.*)
Music.

Full of relief, Mrs Lyons can now be playful.

Use of the middle-class name for mother. This name is also more childlike. Edward is being kept and controlled as a child.

The audience is waiting for the big reveal. The use of dramatic music increases the tension as it would in a film.

Edward's unfinished sentence suggests his distress but also shows his mother's control as he knows his response will not influence her.

 STRETCHIT!

Critics have argued that Willy Russell uses **stereotypical** language features to show the differences between working-class and middle-class characters. How far do you agree? You could think about his use of slang, swearing and shortened words.

Figurative language in the songs

In a recent magazine article, Russell said, 'The kind of theatre I was involved in right from the word go didn't make a distinction between musical and non-musical. When I started work at the Everyman Theatre in Liverpool, it was commonplace to have music as part of your show.'

The play uses realistic dialogue to show characters, with **figurative language** appearing within the songs. Within the songs, we see a return to images that link the themes and messages of the play. Russell also uses music to increase tension within a scene. We have a bass note like a *'heartbeat'* after Mrs Johnstone and Mrs Lyons make their deal. Also *'a note'* punctuates movements in the fight scene in the kitchen with the knife.

Marilyn Monroe

Mrs Johnstone uses the motif of Marilyn Monroe in the opening scene. Here, Marilyn Monroe is used alongside dancing to reveal the impermanence of pleasure and love. Marilyn was a glamorous film star, a symbol of female beauty and sex appeal. This is how Russell presents this impression of Marilyn Monroe in the first song. Mrs Johnstone's husband told her that 'she was sexier than Marilyn Monroe'. However, like the husband's love, these looks don't last, as she becomes 'twice the size of Marilyn Monroe' as her husband leaves her for a younger girl who 'looks a bit like Marilyn Monroe'. In later life, Marilyn Monroe became a victim of her addictions and she died tragically. This aspect of her life is reflected within Mrs Johnstone's songs towards the end of the play. When Mickey is in prison, Mrs Johnstone sings, 'It seems like jail's sent him off the rails,/Just like Marilyn Monroe', reflecting the tragedy that will end the play, just as it ended Marilyn Monroe's life.

Use of metaphor in the songs

The metaphor of 'easy terms' reveals the hardship of Mrs Johnstone's life. The wordplay used by Russell here reflects the 'easy terms' used by finance companies to trap people paying on the 'never-never'. Here companies would charge interest when people bought items on repayment plans. The 'terms' – the interest on the money – would always be high. People would always have to 'pay the price' for their goods, showing how there is no way out of paying what they owe. Here we have a clear link to the theme of fate. 'Easy terms' also refers to the easy relationships that happen between a mother and child. You will have heard of 'being on good terms' with someone. The irony is that Edward is always on good terms with Mrs Johnstone, having an immediate rapport with her. His relationship with Mrs Lyons never shows the 'easy terms' that he has with Mrs Johnstone. It is also ironic that Mrs Johnstone is lamenting that she will not be on 'easy terms' with Edward again. This turns out not to be the case.

Recurring metaphors are used to link the songs and episodes in the storyline. Find another example of this and write a paragraph to show how Russell uses this metaphor in the songs.

Structure

Structure of the play

Blood Brothers takes place in two acts. It has a **cyclical structure** beginning and ending with the scene showing the deaths of two young men. The first act ends with a moment of hope and positivity for the Johnstone family as they are going to move away and have a fresh start – it is their 'bright new day'. Act Two begins by quickly filling in the events of the past seven years. Act Two moves towards a climax of hope and happiness with Mickey and Linda in a relationship before a plot reversal signalling the decline of fortunes for the Johnstone family. This moves to the tragic catastrophe and ending.

Usually in the **denouement**, the characters learn a valuable lesson and reform. What lessons do the characters – and the audience – learn in *Blood Brothers*?

Blood Brothers structure chart

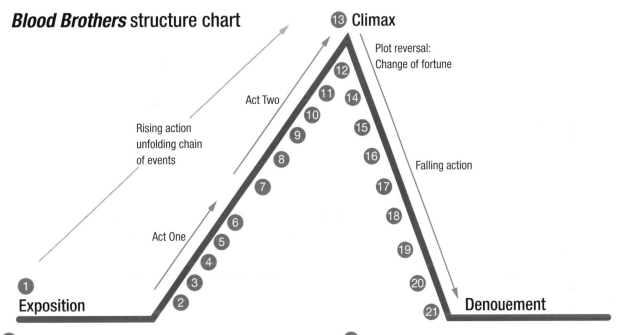

1. **Exposition** – opening – This is the death scene from the end of the play.
2. Inciting incident – Mrs Johnstone gives a baby away to Mrs Lyons.
3. Mrs Lyons sacks Mrs Johnstone.
4. Mickey, Edward and Linda become friends.
5. Edward and Mickey get in trouble with the police.
6. Edward moves away and Mrs Johnstone gives him a locket.
7. The Johnstone family have moved.
8. The boys are suspended from school.
9. Mrs Lyons sees the locket.
10. Edward and Mickey are reunited.
11. Edward and Mickey meet Linda.

12. Edward, Mickey and Linda are firm friends.
13. **Climax** – Linda and Mickey are happy together. Edward is at university.
14. Linda is pregnant and married to Mickey.
15. Mickey is unemployed. Edward tries to give him money.
16. Sammy recruits Mickey for a robbery.
17. Mickey is arrested.
18. Mickey takes antidepressants.
19. **Catastrophe** – Mrs Lyons interferes.
20. **Moment of final suspense** – Mickey has a gun.
21. **Denouement** – This is a return to the opening scene.

 STRETCH**IT!**

Some reviewers suggest that the play has a **linear structure**. Give reasons for and against this argument.

Parallel scenes

The play is structured to show a series of parallels between the working-class, poverty-stricken Johnstone family and the middle-class, wealthy Lyons family. The scenes alternate, showing comparisons and contrasts between the two families, driving home Russell's social message.

Edward and Mickey

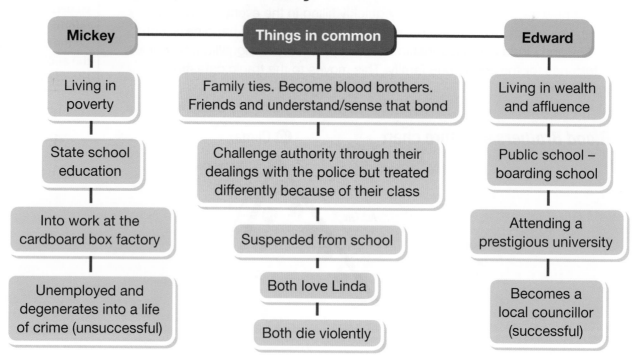

There are many parallels that can be drawn between scenes in the play. Despite the fact that Willy Russell said, 'Blood Brothers is a play that could be played like a tennis match with every scene showing first the working-class situation and then a parallel scene showing the middle-class side of it. The only time I allowed myself to do that was in the scene with the policeman', there are many parallels that can be found and it can be fun looking for them. One such parallel is the teenage Mickey who awkwardly denies his feelings for Linda, his blackhead remover and his 'secret dancing' while Edward is 'awkwardly' waltzing with his mother complaining that he 'hardly ever' sees a girl 'let alone' dances with one.

Design a diagram like the one above to show the parallels between Mrs Johnstone and Mrs Lyons.

AQA exam-style question

'Even if we hadn't seen the deaths of the characters at the start of the play, we know that it will end in tragedy.' How far do you agree with this statement?

Write about:

* how Russell presents the characters in Blood Brothers as tragic figures

* how Russell uses Blood Brothers to explore ideas about social responsibility and fate.

[30 marks]

Staging

The dialogue in *Blood Brothers* is lifelike and very real. However, the staging is often symbolic and stylised. The production notes for the staging of *Blood Brothers* states that the stage should be an 'open stage'. This means there is very little scenery, props or furniture on stage resulting in the action being able to run from one episode to the next without pausing. This enables this two-act play to 'flow easily and smoothly'.

'Two areas on the stage are semi-permanent'. The outside of the Johnstone house and its front door and the comfortable interior of the Lyons' house is shown to the audience. This suggests warmth and comfort that the wealthy Lyons family could afford. In stark contrast, the Johnstone exterior suggests a cold and functional way of life. This lack of scenery means that location is suggested by movement and gesture.

The stylised setting includes how the actors play the characters. Willy Russell explained: 'I always envisioned the children being played by adults. I'd seen plays by John McGrath and Peter Terson in the sixties when twenty-year-old men played five-year-old boys with acceptable realism.'

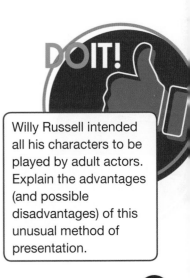

DO IT!

Willy Russell intended all his characters to be played by adult actors. Explain the advantages (and possible disadvantages) of this unusual method of presentation.

Form

Greek tragedy

In a letter written by Willy Russell to Chris Bond, the director of the first production of *Blood Brothers*, he says, '…class splits these two brothers, that class keeps them apart, that class kills them.'

Critics have likened the play to a Greek **tragedy** and it does use many of the features of this type of theatre.

Features of Greek tragedy

- The play is introduced by a **prologue**.

- At the centre of the tragedy there is a tragic hero – a main character.

- The main character has a tragic flaw that brings about their downfall.

- The play often focuses on a family drama.

- The play often contains powerful female characters.

- A chorus comments on the action and the themes of the play.

- Song is often used by the chorus.

- A catastrophe occurs, signalling a change of fortune for the main character.

- Fate predetermines events and there is no escape from it.

Purpose of Greek tragedy

The purpose was to make the audience experience pity or fear in response to pain and suffering to help the audience to get rid of these emotions (catharsis). However, Greek tragedy usually focused on the lives and deaths of great or notable figures whereas Russell depicts the lives of ordinary people.

DOIT!

How does Willy Russell use the elements of Greek tragedy? Write a paragraph to explain your viewpoint.

REVIEW IT!

1   Why do you think Russell starts and ends the play with the deaths of Edward and Mickey?

2   The stage directions describe what should be happening with the music within a scene. Give an example of this.

3   In the parallel scenes with the Policeman, how does he describe Mickey's offence? How does he describe Edward's?

4   Why does Russell use this device in the example of the parallel scene with the Policeman?

5   Give an example of Russell's use of dramatic irony to increase tension.

6   Give an example of Russell's use of music to increase tension.

7   As a seven-year-old, Edward is impressed by Mickey's swearing. What happens when he uses the words himself for the first time?

8   Give an example of a Liverpudlian dialect word used in the play.

9   What does 'living on the Giro' mean?

10 Mickey is married, about to be a father and is unemployed. What parallel life has Edward been living?

11 What does 'cyclical play structure' mean?

12 Explain what makes the dialogue in *Blood Brothers* sound lifelike and real.

13 What 'price' does Mrs Johnstone pay for her 'deal'?

14 What 'price' does Mrs Lyons pay for her 'deal'?

15 What 'price' does Linda pay for her friendship with Mickey and Edward?

16 Could *Blood Brothers* be described as a 'Greek tragedy'? Write a paragraph to explain your ideas.

17 Look at the speech here: 'There are just so many tremendous people'. What class is the character from? How do you know?

18 Explain how Russell uses language to show the Liverpool accent.

19 How would this line of dialogue by Mickey be written in Standard English? 'Come on, bunk under y' fence, y' Ma won't see y'.'

20 Who would you describe as the hero of *Blood Brothers*?

Doing well in your AQA exam

Understanding the question

NAILIT!

Read the question carefully and understand it. Make sure you focus on answering the question. Don't just write whatever you know about the play. Your answer must be relevant to the question.

Carefully preparing to answer the exam question is vital. If you are not clear in your mind about what the question is asking for, then there is a real risk that your answer will include irrelevant ideas and evidence.

Below is an AQA exam-style question. The question itself has been prepared by a student so that they fully understand it. Look at their notes.

What admirable or heroic qualities do these women demonstrate?

How does Russell make us feel about these characters?

AQA exam-style question

How far do you agree that Russell presents women as heroes in Blood Brothers?

Write about:

What heroic or admirable qualities might we expect to see?

Differences between the presentation of working-class and middle-class women.

- how Russell presents the female characters in the play

- how Russell uses the female characters to explore ideas about heroism.

What methods and techniques does Russell use?

Do the men demonstrate heroic qualities?

This student has studied the question carefully and realised that:

- the focus is on the heroism *and* whether the women characters demonstrate admirable or heroic qualities

- 'presents' means how Russell creates and shapes the characters' speech and behaviour to explore this idea by identifying specific literary techniques

- the idea of heroism needs to be explored in the answer from three different viewpoints: the setting of the 1960s, the viewpoint of a 1980s, audience and the viewpoint of a modern audience

- what we think and feel about the characters has been shaped and controlled by Russell.

'Pinning the question down' in this way has allowed the student to make sure that they have really thought about what the question is asking. In the examination room it is very easy to misread questions, answering the question that you want or expect to see, rather than the question that is actually there. The method outlined here will support you as you begin to find some useful ideas to support your answer.

DOIT!

Choose another question from earlier in this guide. 'Pin the question down' as above.

Planning your answer

NAILIT!

High-level answers should have an over-arching **argument** that is developed through the essay.

You have 45 minutes for your response; 5–10 minutes spent preparing the question and planning your answer is time well used. It will help make sure your answer is clear and relevant. Practise preparing and planning as part of your revision programme.

Once you have pinned down your question properly, planning an answer will be quite straightforward. Your brief plan should set out:

- your key, *relevant* ideas
- the content of each of four or five paragraphs
- the order of the paragraphs.

Here is the same student's plan for the question on page 84. They have allowed 10 minutes for planning and 35 minutes for writing.

Paragraph	Content	Timing plan
1	Brief introduction: use the words of the question and 'pinning the question down' to establish the focus of the answer and develop a line of argument.	9.15am
2	Mrs Johnstone's presentation as a hero. Always keeps going. Is not defeated by the tragedy at the end of the play.	9.17am
3	Linda's admirable qualities and how Russell develops her character so as to make her believable.	9.24am
4	Mrs Lyons as a different type of woman: only concerned for her own needs.	9.31am
5	ways in which Mrs Johnstone/Linda are not heroic/admirable.	9.38am
6	Brief conclusion. Refer back to question. Men - do any characters show admirable qualities? Check answer.	9.45am

Sticking to the plan

Note how this student has jotted down time points for when they should move on to the next section of their answer. That way, they make sure they do not get stuck on one point and fail to cover the question focus in enough breadth.

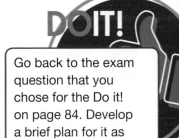

DOIT!

Go back to the exam question that you chose for the Do it! on page 84. Develop a brief plan for it as above.

Planning to meet the mark scheme

The plan above suggests that the student has thought carefully about the task in the question, that they are familiar with the mark scheme for their AQA Paper Two Modern Texts question and are planning to cover its requirements:

Assessment objective	What the plan promises
AO1 (Response to task and text)	Planning focuses on the question and the how the women are/are not presented as heroes. Some personal responses to be included.
AO2 (Identification of writer's methods)	Russell's language choices to present Mrs Johnstone's qualities. How we view Mrs Lyon's selfishness. Language used by Linda to show her as positive and supportive of Mickey.
AO3 (understanding of ideas/perspectives/context)	Links to themes of fate, social class and justice. Links to Russell's message. Consideration of how a 1980s' audience and a modern audience would consider the women.

(See the mark scheme on pages 86–87.)

What your AQA examiner is looking for

Your answer will be marked according to a mark scheme based on four assessment objectives (AOs). The AOs focus on specific knowledge, understanding and skills. AO4 – which is about vocabulary, sentence structures, spelling and punctuation – is worth just four marks. Together, the other AOs are worth 30 marks, so it is important to understand what the examiner is looking out for.

Mark scheme

Your AQA examiner will mark your answers in 'bands'. These bands loosely equate as follows:

- band 6 approx. grades 8 and 9
- band 5 approx. grades 6 and 7
- band 4 approx. grades 5 and 6
- band 3 approx. grades 3 and 4
- band 2 approx. grades 1 and 2.

Most importantly, the improvement descriptors in the table below will help you understand how to improve your answers and, therefore, gain more marks. The maximum number of marks for each AO is shown.

Assessment objective (AO)		Improvement descriptors				
		Band 2 Your answer…	**Band 3** Your answer…	**Band 4** Your answer…	**Band 5** Your answer…	**Band 6** Your answer…
AO1 12 marks	**Read, understand and respond**	is relevant and backs up ideas with references to the play.	often explains the play in relation to the question.	clearly explains the play in relation to the question.	thoughtfully explains the play in relation to the question.	critically explores the play in relation to the question.
	Use evidence	makes some comments about these references.	refers to details in the play to back up points.	carefully chooses close references to the play to back up points.	thoughtfully builds appropriate references into points.	chooses precise details from the play to clinch points.
AO2 12 marks	**Language, form and structure**	mentions some of Russell's methods.	comments on some of Russell's methods, and their effects.	clearly explains Russell's key methods, and their effects.	thoughtfully explores Russell's methods, and their effects.	analyses Russell's methods, and how these influence the audience.
	Subject terminology	sometimes refers to subject terminology.	uses some relevant terminology.	helpfully uses varied, relevant terminology.	makes thoughtful use of relevant terminology.	chooses subject terminology to make points precise and convincing.
AO3 6 marks	**Contexts**	makes some simple inferences about contexts.	infers Russell's point of view and the significance of contexts.	shows a clear appreciation of Russell's point of view and the significance of contexts.	explores Russell's point of view and the significance of relevant contexts.	makes perceptive and revealing links between the play and relevant contexts.

AO1 Read, understand and respond/Use evidence

Make sure you read and answer the question carefully. The examiner will be looking for evidence that you have answered the question given. Do not make the mistake of going into the exam with an answer in mind. Knowing the play well will give you the confidence to show your understanding of the play and its ideas as you answer the question on the paper in front of you.

Using evidence means supporting your ideas with references to the play. They can be indirect references – brief mentions of an event or what a character says or does – or direct references – quotations. Choose and use evidence carefully so that it really does support a point you are making. Quotations should be as short as possible, and the very best ones are often neatly built into your writing.

AO2: Language, form and structure/Subject terminology

Remember that *Blood Brothers* is not real life. It is a play that Russell has *created* to entertain and influence the audience. The language and other methods he uses have been chosen carefully for effect. Good answers will not just point out good words Russell has used: they will explore the effects of those word choices on the audience. You must refer to the writer, showing that you understand that the play is a construct at all times, to progress beyond Grade 3.

Subject terminology is about choosing your words carefully, using the right words and avoiding vague expressions. It is also about using terminology *helpfully*. For example, here are two different uses of subject terminology, the first much more useful than the second:

Student answer A

During the whole of this song, use of the repeated 'the devil's got your number' ensures the audience understands that past actions will catch up with the characters and they cannot escape.

Student answer B

The Narrator uses repetition when he says, 'the devil's got your number'.

AO3: Contexts

Notice the emphasis on 'relevant contexts' higher up the mark criteria. The best answers will include contextual information that is directly relevant to the question, not just the play in general. (See answer A on page 74 for a good example.) Consider how might:

- the society Russell lived in have influenced his ideas and attitudes?

- the society you live in influence how you respond to ideas and attitudes in the play?

- knowledge of the whole play enrich your understanding of a particular part of the play?

AO4: Vocabulary, sentence structures, spelling and punctuation

Make sure that you use a range of vocabulary and sentence structures for clarity, purpose and effect. Accurate spelling and punctuation is important too for this assessment objective.

NAILIT!

To boost your marks when answering questions do the following:

- Know the play well. Read it and study it.

- Don't go into the exam with ready-prepared answers.

- Read the question and make sure you answer it thoughtfully.

- Choose details in the play that will support your points.

- Don't treat the play and its characters as though they are real. Instead ask why Russell has chosen to create those words, or that event. What effect is he trying to achieve?

NAILIT!

Introductions and conclusions are not essential. Write them only if they help you to answer the question. However, higher-grade answers signal a clear line of argument in their opening sentences.

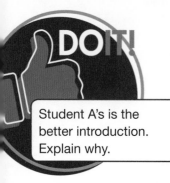

Student A's is the better introduction. Explain why.

Writing your answer

Getting started

You have looked at one student's plan, and you will have noticed that they have decided to write a short introduction. Here are the openings of two students' answers to the question on page 84 about how Russell presents women as heroes in *Blood Brothers*.

Student answer A

Russell explores the role of women through his presentation of three very different women in the play - Mrs Johnstone, Mrs Lyons and Linda. Through these women, and the contrasting reactions to them Russell provokes in the audience, we encounter women both as heroes and as villains, so that while there are female heroes in the play, it isn't clear that you have to be female to be heroic - or heroic to be female!

Student answer B

I am going to write about how Russell presents women in 'Blood Brothers'. First I am going to talk about Mrs Johnstone. Then I am going to talk about Mrs Lyons. The play begins in the 1960s but it was written in about 1980 and things have changed a lot since those days. Those are the sorts of things I'm going to write about in my answer.

The response

Look at the student's plan for their essay on page 85. Here is most of the second paragraph of their answer. Note the way they use very brief quotations to help them comment on Russell's methods and their effects. An examiner has made some comments in the margin.

Overall, Russell presents Mrs Johnstone as a hero with a number of qualities the audience cannot help admire. Despite all her hardships and bad luck, she always picks herself up and keeps going. Even at the end of the play when she has just suffered a terrible tragedy, we get the impression that she is not going to give in to self-pity and defeatism. Her imperative verb, 'say', when she tells us to 'say it's just a dream' expresses her determination to blot out the crushing reality of the double shooting and to convince herself that the tragedy was not real but part of 'an old movie'. The audience might not see her as heroic to delude herself, but we already know that Mrs Johnstone can cope with reality. Her whole approach to life's problems is realistic and practical. Her desire to identify with Marilyn Monroe is a desire to identify with glamour - not a perfect glamour, but one that is mixed with pain and struggle....

The words of the question are used to keep a focus on what is being asked.

Direct evidence used – and built neatly into student's own words.

Effect of words is identified and analysed closely.

Using words from the question to keep on track.

Focus on context and audience reaction.

Confident focus on Russell's methods.

Paragraph topics

The rest of your paragraphs should each deal with a subtopic of the main focus of the question. Here, the question focuses on Russell's presentation of women as heroes. The student's plan suggests that the next four paragraph topics will be: Linda's admirable qualities and how Russell develops her character so as to make her believable; Mrs Lyons as a different type of woman; ways in which Mrs Johnstone/Linda are *not* heroic/admirable; men. There is a balance of paragraph topics here, allowing the student to both agree and disagree with the question focus, thus allowing them to answer the question in an open, exploring way.

Don't forget the writer's purpose

Blood Brothers is not real life: it has been constructed by the writer for a purpose. Below is another part of the same student's answer. Notice how the student points out what Willy Russell has deliberately done – and why. These references are underlined to point them out.

> Heroism usually involves self essness, but Mrs Lyons seems only to be concerned about her own needs. <u>The way Russell presents her</u> makes it hard for the audience to sympathise with her. When Mrs Johnstone admires her 'lovely house', Mrs Lyons moans that it is too large, and very often in the play she seems insensitive to Mrs Johnstone's poverty and ungrateful for the advantages she is lucky enough to have. However, perhaps because Willy Russell was brought up among women and spent five years as a ladies' hairdresser, <u>he even arouses compassion</u> for an unattractive character like Mrs Lyons, so when she says she has 'been trying for such a long time' to have a baby, <u>Russell's use of</u> the word 'such' simply and powerfully expresses the genuine unhappiness she is suffering.

Using evidence:

This student uses **direct evidence** in the form of quotations when they know them and uses **indirect evidence** by referring to the kind of words used when they are uncertain of the whole quotation. Both forms of evidence are valid.

Ending your answer

If you write a conclusion, make it useful: don't simply repeat what you have already said. The answer we have been looking at ends with this summary:

> On balance, I think that Russell presents women as 'heroic'. Even Mrs Lyons has admirable qualities. Mickey has some heroic qualities too: he fights to rise out of the poverty and crime of his upbringing. Perhaps the real point Russell is making is that there are no real heroes – just ordinary people who make the very best of what they've got.

Use the preparation and planning you did for your chosen exam question (see page 84) to write a full answer.

 STRETCHIT!

Develop a range of evaluative vocabulary to enable you to pinpoint Russell's intention. Use words like:

- condemns
- criticises
- exposes
- ridicules
- subverts
- questions

Going for the top grades

Of course you will always try to write the best answer possible, but if you are aiming for the top grades then it is vital to be clear about what examiners will be looking out for. The best answers will tend to:

• show a clear understanding of both the play *and* the exam question • show insight into the play and the question focus • explore the play in relation to the focus of the question • choose evidence precisely and wisely	**AO1**
• analyse Russell's methods and their effect • use relevant, helpful subject terminology	**AO2**
• explore aspects of context that are relevant to the play and the question	**AO3**

A great answer **will not** waste words or use evidence for its own sake.

A great answer **will** show that you are engaging directly and thoughtfully with the play, not just scribbling down everything you have been told about it.

The best answers will be RIPE with ideas and engagement:

R	Relevant	Stay strictly relevant to the question.
I	Insightful	Develop relevant insights into the play, its characters and themes.
P	Precise	Choose and use evidence precisely so that it strengthens your points.
E	Exploratory	Explore relevant aspects of the play, looking at it from more than one angle.

Below is part of a student's answer to: What ideas about inequality does Russell explore in the play *Blood Brothers*? The student is developing an original line of thought: are working-class characters in the play necessarily interested in equality? Next to the answer are some comments by an examiner.

DO IT!

Find an essay or practice answer you have written about *Blood Brothers*.

Use the advice and examples on this page to help you decide how your writing could be improved.

If Russell had wanted us to be on the side of the working class, then why didn't he make all his working-class characters act responsibly and support each other? Even Mrs Johnstone plans reckless purchases from the catalogue - bikes, Meccano sets, etc. - things her family could do without, thus worsening her own position and putting the Milkman and the Catalogue Man under unnecessary moral pressure. However, worse still is the way Russell has these fellow members of the working class almost enjoying Mrs Johnstone's deprivation: the Milkman makes crass jokes about randy wives and milkmen and the Finance Man enjoys giving her a harsh lecture punctuated by aggressive swearing - 'bloody'. Russell's picture of working-class behaviour is not at all attractive, but then perhaps he is suggesting that it is inequality that makes people turn on each other rather than sticking together.

Original insight related to class context.

Complexities of Mrs Johnstone's behaviour pointed out.

Use of indirect references to illustrate points.

Precise evidence neatly integrated into argument.

Tentatively introduced insight/ hypothesis.

Good return to question focus to maintain relevance.

REVIEW IT!

1 In your exam, how long should you spend preparing, planning and writing your *Blood Brothers* answer?

2 Other than *Blood Brothers*, what texts will you need to write about in Paper 2 (Modern texts)?

3 How many *Blood Brothers* questions will be on the paper?

4 How many questions should you answer on *Blood Brothers*?

5 Here is a template for an essay question for *Blood Brothers*. Create your own exam questions by filling in the brackets.

How and why does [name of character] change in *Blood Brothers*?
Write about:
- how [name of character] responds to other characters
- how Willy Russell presents [name of character] by the way he writes.

6 Here is a template for an essay question for *Blood Brothers*. Create your own exam questions by filling in the brackets.

How does Willy Russell explore [theme] in *Blood Brothers*?
Write about:
- the ideas about [name of theme] in *Blood Brothers*
- how Willy Russell presents these ideas in the way he writes.

7 Here is a template for an essay question for *Blood Brothers*. Create your own exam questions by filling in the brackets.

Do you think [name of character] is an important character in *Blood Brothers*? Write about:
- how Willy Russell presents [name of character]
- how Willy Russell uses [name of character] to present ideas about [theme].

8 How long should you spend planning and preparing your answer?

9 Why is it important to prepare or 'pin down' your exam question?

10 What is meant by an indirect reference to the play?

11 Why is it helpful to check your vocabulary, sentence structures, spelling and punctuation during your exam?

12 How many marks are AO1, 2 and 3 worth together?

13 What does AO1 test? How many marks are allocated out of 30?

14 What does AO2 test? How many marks are allocated out of 30?

15 Your friend has told you that they are going to learn an essay that they wrote in the mock exams as their revision. What would you say to them?

16 'Introductions and conclusions are not essential.' Is this true or false?

17 In the month leading up to your exam, what is a useful strategy to help you with your revision?

18 Plan a five-paragraph answer to the question you created in question 5 above.
(Or you could use this question: Do you think Linda is an important character in *Blood Brothers*?
Write about:
- how Willy Russell presents Linda
- how Willy Russell uses Linda to present ideas about people and society.)

19 Plan a five-paragraph answer to the question you created for question 6 in this Review it! quiz
(or you could use this question: How does Russell explore family relationships in *Blood Brothers*?
Write about:
- ideas about family relationships in *Blood Brothers*
- how Willy Russell presents these relationships in the way he writes.)

20 Use the plan you made in question 18 or 19 above to write an answer in no more than 40 minutes.

NAIL IT!

In the month leading up to the exam, all your revision should be based on planning and writing answers to exam questions. You will find plenty of exam questions in this guide for practice.

AQA exam-style questions

NAILIT!

Make sure that you only answer *one* question in your examination. The examiner will only give you marks for one answer.

On these pages you will find five practice questions for *Blood Brothers.* In your exam you must choose one question to answer from a choice of two. Quite often you will be presented with a question that focuses on character and a question that focuses on a theme or idea. Sometimes a question will focus on both (see question 3 below). Self-assessment guidance is provided on the app/online.

PRACTICE QUESTION 1

How far does Russell present Mickey as a likeable character?

Write about:

- the way Mickey changes throughout the play
- how Russell presents Mickey by the way he writes about him.

[30 marks]
AO4 [4 marks]

PRACTICE QUESTION 2

How does Russell present different attitudes to poverty and social class?

Write about:

- what the different characters' attitudes are to poverty and social class
- how Russell presents attitudes towards poverty and social class by the way he writes.

[30 marks]
AO4 [4 marks]

PRACTICE QUESTION 3

How does Russell use the Narrator to explore ideas about responsibility?

Write about:

- how Russell presents the character of the Narrator
- how Russell uses the Narrator to explore ideas about responsibility.

[30 marks]
AO4 [4 marks]

PRACTICE QUESTION 4

How does Russell present Mr Lyons?

Write about:

- how Mr Lyons responds to his family and to other characters
- how Russell presents Mr Lyons by the way he writes.

[30 marks]
AO4 [4 marks]

PRACTICE QUESTION 5

'*Blood Brothers* is a play about relationships.' How far do you agree with this statement?

Write about:

- how Russell presents the different relationships within the play
- how Russell uses relationships to explore other important ideas.

[30 marks]
AO4 [4 marks]

DO IT!

Look at these five questions. Rank the questions from the question with which you are most comfortable to the one with which you are least comfortable.

Are there any patterns that you notice? For example, do you prefer character question or theme questions?

Are there any gaps in your knowledge of the text? Go back and review those areas

STRETCH IT!

Choose the question that you find most difficult. Use this guide and your notes to plan an answer to it.

Glossary

accent The way someone pronounces the words and letters of their language. Different areas of a country – for example, Liverpool – have their own distinctive accent.

adjective A word that describes a noun (for example: *dreadful* note; *restless* ecstasy).

alliteration Words starting with the same sound and placed near each other for **effect** (for example: Mr Lyons calling Miss Jones a 'perfect poppet', thus patronising her).

cast All the actors who play the **characters** in a performance.

character A person in a play or story: a person created by the writer (for example: Mickey, Mrs Lyons, Linda).

characteristic The words or actions a writer gives a **character**.

connotation The implied (see **implicit** also) meaning of a word or **phrase**. For example, the word mob means a large group of people, but it implies violence. If someone dashes down the road, we know that they are moving quickly, but that choice of word also implies urgency. A connotation is sometimes called a nuance.

context The circumstances in which a play was written or is watched. These could include normal beliefs at the turn of the 17th century, or the typical attitudes of a 21st-century audience.

cyclical structure A storyline that ends at the same place or point that it begins.

denouement The final part of a play or narrative in which the strands of the plot are drawn together and events are explained or resolved.

dialect The grammar and vocabulary typically used in a particular part of the country (for example: Liverpool) or by a particular group of people – such as bakers, middle-class people, and so on.

dialogue The words that **characters** say in plays or in fiction. In a playscript a character's lines of dialogue are indicated with the character's name.

director The person who prepares a play for performance. They are responsible for decisions about the acting, lighting, scenery and so on.

effect The impact that a writer's or **character's** words have on the audience: the mood, feeling or reaction the words create in the audience.

figurative language Language that is not literal. Common forms of figurative language include **similes** and **metaphors**.

foreshadow A clue or a warning about a future event.

fourth wall The fourth wall of the stage is the audience, who can see the action, yet the **characters** cannot 'see' the audience. The 'fourth wall' draws attention to the illusion of reality that is happening on stage. Of course, not all plays are performed on a stage with the audience forming a 'fourth wall' in front.

hyperbole Over the top, exaggerated language (for example: *wretched*).

interpret Use clues to work out meanings or the feelings or motives of a **character**.

irony 1 Mild sarcasm. A technique sometimes used by writers to mock a **character** and make them appear ridiculous or dishonest. 2 An event or result that seems to be the opposite of what could reasonably be expected. This causes a sort of bitter amusement to the victim. For example, it is ironic that the only time Mickey ever fires a gun accurately is when he does it by mistake with fatal results.

linear structure The order in which events are presented corresponds to the order in which they happen.

metaphor Comparing two things by referring to them as though they are the same thing (for example: Mr Johnstone tells Mrs Johnstone that her 'eyes were deep blue pools'. They were not literally deep blue pools.).

motif Something with a symbolic meaning that is repeated throughout a text or play to establish a theme or certain mood. A motif can be almost anything (for example: an idea, an object, a concept, a **character** type, the weather).

narrator A storyteller. It is unusual to have a Narrator in a play, but Russell uses one to summarise parts of the story and to comment on the action.

personification A **metaphor** that represents a thing as a living creature: for example, the **Narrator** personifies fate as a dealer of cards.

phrase A group of words within a sentence.

(play)script The words written by the playwright for the actors to perform.

prologue An introduction to a play, usually spoken by some sort of **narrator** or chorus (group of speakers).

rhyme Words chosen by a poet or song writer because they have the same sound (for example: *he/flea*; *stable/label*; *laughter/after*).

simile Describing something by comparing it with something else (for example: Edward and Mickey are 'as like...as two new pins'; Mr Johnstone told Mrs Johnstone that her skin was 'as soft as snow.').

slang Informal expressions that would be considered unacceptable in formal situations (for example: Sammy's description of Edward as 'a friggin' poshy'.)

spoiler Details which give away the ending of a play, film or other story. *Blood Brothers* is unusual in that the ending is given away at the start.

stage directions These are the instructions that a playwright puts into a script for the benefit of actors and **directors**. Usually these appear in the script in *italics* or in (brackets).

stereotype A **character** who is created not as an interesting individual, but as a type. For example, Mr Lyons is in many respects a stereotype of a particular sort of man: he makes sexist assumptions about the roles of men and women.

structure The way in which the events in a text or play are ordered. For example, *Blood Brothers* is arranged into two acts; it borrows the forms of ancient Greek **tragedy**; it has repeated lines in songs.

symbol(ise) A symbol is something that represents something else. Using symbols can be a way for the author to influence a reader without their realising (for example, at the fairground the rifle range man/**Narrator** sings of lambs to symbolise the friends' youthful innocence and naivety).

sympathetic A sympathetic **character** is one that the writer creates in such a way that the audience *feels* for them – sympathises with them.

tone The mood of a text, or the attitude of the author or **narrator** towards the topic. Tones can be mocking, affectionate, polite, authoritative and so on.

tragedy A form of drama in which a hero's life ends in disaster, normally through a combination of bad luck, fate, and their own personal weaknesses. Tragedy as a play form shows that human beings are fragile when faced with suffering, especially as this suffering is caused by human and divine actions; in a tragedy, the main **character** will die at the end usually because of a mistake they have made or through an error in judgement – their tragic flaw.

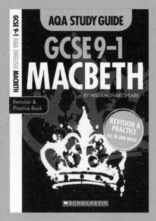
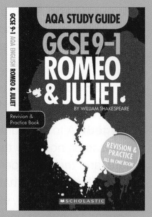
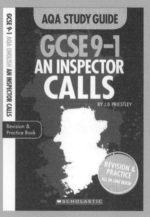
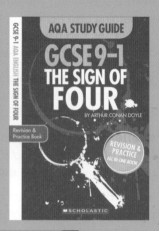
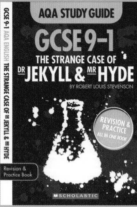

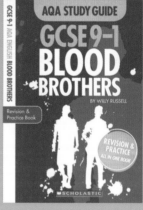